The Gift of
'The 7 Realms'

*A Newfound Pathway **to Higher Spiritual Consciousness***

A 12-Week *Master Course* Workbook in
Mindfulness and Meditation

The Pyramid of Sovereignty

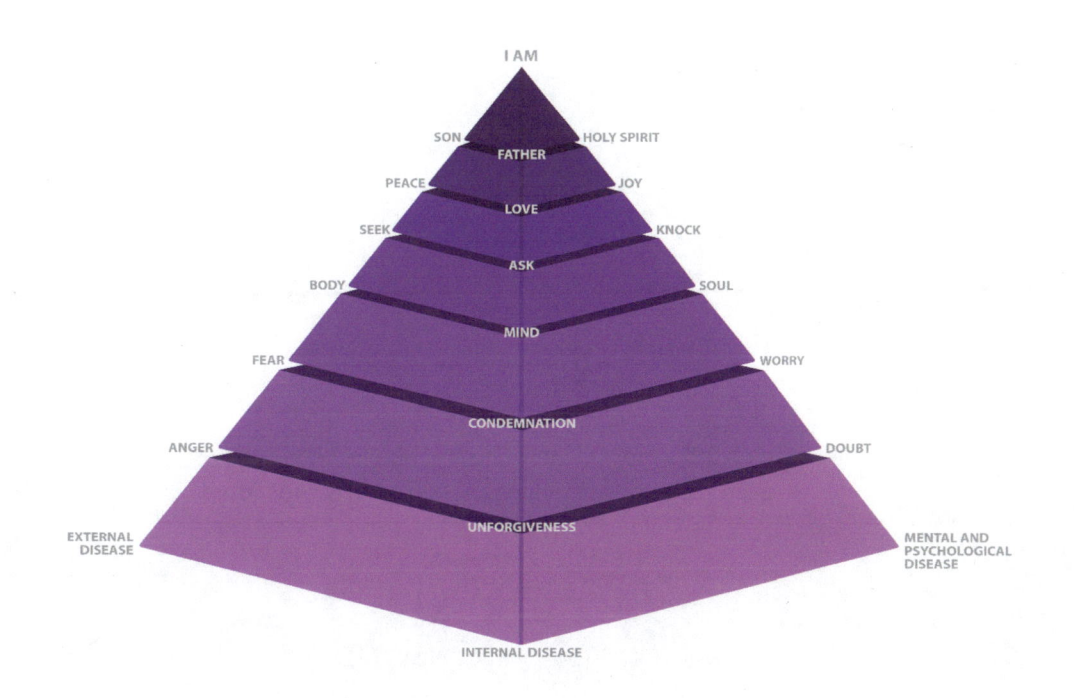

Ryan C. Neal, MD

A physician's journey from traditional medicine to the discovery of a new pathway to higher consciousness and spiritual wellness through Christian Mindfulness and Biblical Meditation

ABOVE CONSCIOUSNESS PUBLISHING

ISBN 979-8-9912763-0-6

All scripture quotes and references are taken
from the public domain unless otherwise specified.

'The7Realms': The Workbook

© 2024 Ryan C. Neal, MD

Copyright notice: All rights reserved under the International and Pan-American Copyright Conventions. No part of this book may be reproduced or transmitted in any form or by any means, electronic or mechanical, including photocopying, recording, or by any information storage and retrieval system, without permission in writing from the publisher.

Warning: the unauthorized reproduction or distribution of this copyrighted work is illegal. Criminal copyright infringement, including infringement without monetary gain, is investigated by the FBI and is punishable by up to 5 years in prison and a fine of $250,000.

'The 7 Realms'
The Workbook

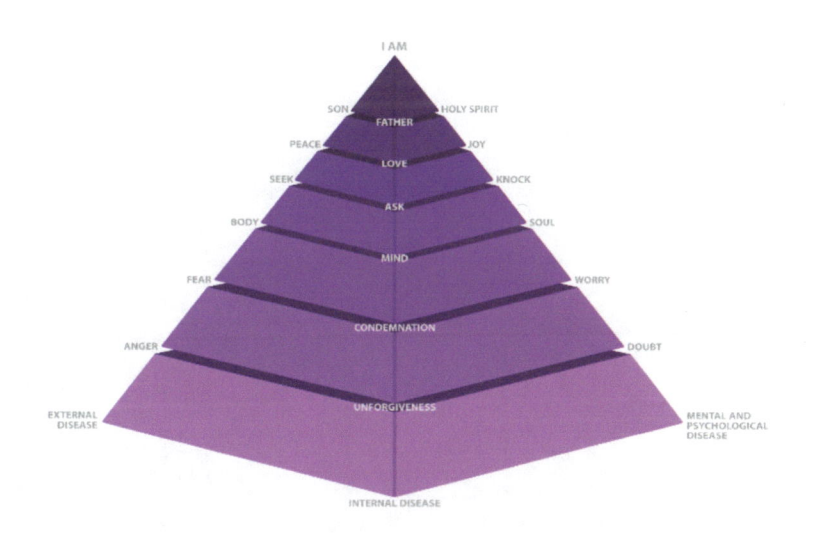

The Pyramid of Sovereignty

(The Primary Pyramid)

Dedication and Acknowledgements

I dedicate this book to my late mother (Nana), for always making me believe I could do anything.

I want to thank my children Mallory, Chris (Ryan Jr.), and Brandi for their belief in me and my unusual ideas.

To my grandchildren Jayden and Jaxson for making me their superhero.

To my wife, Beth, for her love and dedication to endure my constant rewrites and self-critiquing.

To my siblings, Angela, Alicia, and Eric for their edits and inspirations.

And last but never least, to you, the reader. I hope this labor of love helps you on your journey to higher consciousness and spiritual well-beingness.

My Physician Statement

As a physician, I am keenly aware of the physical, genetic, environmental, and psychosocial factors that contribute to physical illness.

It is paramount to stress that I am a staunch advocate for appropriate medical management across all disease categories.

Nothing in this workbook should replace the recommendations and treatments provided by your personal physicians.

However, addressing only the physical aspects of illness without considering spiritual needs is not the most effective approach. A complementary and holistic approach is always preferred.

As a student of Spiritual Consciousness, Christian Mindfulness, and Biblical Meditation, I have recognized the positive impact of mindfulness and meditation in managing disease.

Through the principles outlined in 'The7Realms', I have discovered a method to alleviate much of the pain and suffering associated with physical illness and the negative spiritual consciousness that contributes to unwell thoughts, feelings, and emotions.

I share these insights in The Gift of 'The7Realms'.

-R.C. Neal, MD

Contents

Preface: What is 'The7Realms'? 1

The Co-creation of 'The7Realms' 7

How To Use 'The7Realms' Workbook 12

Glossary- Contextual Definition for 'The7Realms' 15

Week 1/Lesson 1: Introduction- Spiritual Consciousness and Spiritual Energy 24

1.1- The Divine Right of Spiritual Wellness 26

1.2- My Story- God, Science, and Math 28

1.3- The Powerful Discovery of Trilateral Words and Scriptures 33

1.4 -Christian Mindfulness and Biblical Meditation 37

1.5-Definition of Consciousness, Spiritual Consciousness, and Spiritual Wellness 39

1.6-Spiritual Energy and Consciousness Travel 45

1.7-The Energy of Consciousness 49

1.8-The Energy/Power of the Visualized, the Heard, and the Spoken Word 52

1.9-Thoughts, Feelings, and Emotions (TFEs) 55

1.10-Prayer and Meditation Evoke Higher Spiritual Energy 58

Questions for Week 1/Lesson 1 61

Week 2/Lesson 2: Consciousness Levels and Spiritual Realms 69

2.1- The 3 Levels of Consciousness 71

2.2- The Structure and Organization of The Seven Realms of Spiritual Consciousness- The Pyramid of Sovereignty 74

2.3- Levels of Consciousness and the Bi-directional Flow of Spiritual Consciousness 79

2.4- The Explanation of Consciousness Travel or Transcending from Lower Consciousness 82

2.5- Spiritual Entropy and Quantum Mechanics 85

2.6- Spiritual Energy and Vibrational Frequency of Consciousness 88

2.7- Examples of Trilateral Words and Scriptures 92

Questions for Week 2/Lesson 2 98

Week 3/Lesson 3: The Seven Realms 106

3.1- The Seven Realms 108

3.2- The Pyramid of Sovereignty -The Primary Pyramid 111

3.3- The Seven Realms of The Pyramid of Sovereignty 113

3.4- The 7 Discoveries Related to the Energy and Power of Trilateral Words and Scriptures of the Bible in 'The7Realms' 130

Questions for Week 3/Lesson 3.. 132

Week 4/Lesson 4: The First Realm- The Trinity **140**

4.1- The First Trilateral Realm 142

4.2- The Corresponding Scriptures for The Trinity: God the Father, God the Son, and God the Holy Spirit... 145

4.3- The Definitions of God the Father, God the Son, and God the Holy Spirit................................ 147

4.4- The Doctrine of The Trinity.. 149

4.5- The Spiritual and Biblical Definition of God the Father, God the Son, and God the Holy Spirit .. 152

The Exercise- The Mindfulness and Meditation Practice for The First Realm................................ 155

Questions for Week 4/Lesson 4... 158

Week 5/Lesson 5: The Second Realm- The Fruit of The Spirit **166**

5.1- The Second Trilateral Realm.. 168

5.2- The Corresponding Scriptures for The Realm of The Fruit of The Spirit: Love, Peace, and Joy ... 171

5.3- Understanding The Fruit of The Spirit- Love, Peace, and Joy in 'The7Realms' 173

5.4- The Standard and the Biblical Definitions of Love, Peace, and Joy.. 176

The Exercise- The Mindfulness and Meditation Practice for The Second Realm............................. 180

Questions for Week 5/Lesson 5... 183

Week 6/Lesson 6: The Third Realm- Manifestation..**191**

6.1- The Third Trilateral Realm 193

6.2- The Corresponding Scriptures for The Realm of Manifestation: Ask, Seek, and Knock............... 196

6.3- Understanding Manifestation: Ask, Seek, and Knock in 'The7Realms' 198

6.4- The Standard and the Biblical Definitions of Ask, Seek, and Knock 201

The Exercise- The Mindfulness and Meditation Practice for The Third Realm 206

Questions for Week 6/Lesson 6... 209

Week 7/Lesson 7: The Fourth Realm- The Realm of Middle Consciousness.....................................**217**

7.1- The Fourth Trilateral Realm.. 219

7.2- The Corresponding Scriptures for The Middle Realm of Consciousness: Mind, Body, and Soul . 222

7.3- Understanding the Concept of Mind, Body, and Soul in 'The7Realms' 224

7.4- The Biblical and Spiritual Concepts of Mind, Body, and Soul.. 226

The Exercise- The Mindfulness and Meditation Practice for The Fourth Realm............................... 232

Questions for Week 7/Lesson 7... 235

Week 8/Lesson 8: The Fifth Realm- Condemnation, Fear, and Worry **243**

8.1- The Fifth Trilateral Realm 245

8.2- The Corresponding Scriptures for The Realm of Condemnation, Fear, and Worry 248

8.3- Understanding the Concepts of Condemnation, Fear, and Worry in 'The7Realms' 250

8.4- Contemplating the Biblical and Spiritual Concepts of Condemnation, Fear, and Worry 254

The Exercise- The Mindfulness and Meditation Practice for The Fifth Realm 260

Questions for Week 8/Lesson 8 263

Week 9/Lesson 9: The Sixth Realm- Unforgiveness, Anger, and Doubt 271

9.1- The Sixth Trilateral Realm The Realm of Unforgiveness, Anger, and Doubt 273

9.2- The Corresponding Scriptures for The Realm of Unforgiveness, Anger, and Doubt 276

9.3- Understanding the Concepts of Unforgiveness, Anger, and Doubt in 'The7Realms' 278

9.4- Contemplating the Biblical and Spiritual Concepts of Unforgiveness, Anger, and Doubt 280

Questions for Week 9/Lesson 9 288

Week 10/ Lesson 10: The Seventh Realm- Disease Manifestation 296

10.1- The Seventh Trilateral Realm 298

10.2- The Corresponding Scriptures for The Realm of Internal, External, and Mental/Psychological Diseases 301

10.3- Understanding the Concepts of Internal, External, and Mental/Psychological Diseases in 'The7Realms' 304

10.4- Contemplating the Biblical and Spiritual Concepts of Internal, External, and Mental Diseases . 311

The Exercise- The Mindfulness and Meditation Practice for The Seventh Realm 315

Questions for Week 10/Lesson 10 320

Week 11/ Lesson 11: The Anchoring, Opening and Transitioning Mantras of 'The7Realms'- The Inner Hum, The Amen, and The Breath 328

11.1- Anchoring- The Inner Hum 330

11.2- The Opening Mantra- The Amen 335

11.3- Transitioning- The Breath 339

Questions for Week 11/Lesson 11 343

Week 12/ Lesson 12: Conclusion- The Step-by-Step Explanation of The Meditation Process - 'The7Realms' Meditation 351

12.1- The Practice of 'The7Realms' in Mindfulness and Meditation 353

12.2- The Structure and Organization of The Seven Realms of Spiritual Consciousness: 355

12.3- An Overview of How to Use 'The7Realms' Mindfulness and Meditation Practice 358

12.4- Examples of Anchoring Prayer(s)- Let's Begin… 368

12.5- The Comprehensive Practice of 'The7Realms'-STEP 1- Identify the Realm of Spiritual Consciousness You Exist in Now and Start the Meditation Process Here 371

12.6- The Comprehensive Practice of 'The7Realms'-STEP 2 - Transition to The Realm of Middle Consciousness- Becoming Conscious 376

12.7- The Comprehensive Practice of 'The7Realms'-STEP 3- Final Step: Transcend- Choose Which Realm of Higher Consciousness You Wish to Attain and Transcend to this Realm 381

Questions for Week 12/Lesson 12 386

In Closing: Uncovering the Patterns of Trilateral Words in The Bible 394

Ryan C. Neal, MD

Preface: What is 'The7Realms'?

What is 'The7Realms'?

The Seven *Trilateral* Realms of Spiritual Consciousness (aka 'The7Realms') is a newly discovered and divinely organized pathway to Higher Spiritual Consciousness through the Mindfulness and Meditation practice of 'The7Realms'. This transformative discovery unveils 84 *trilateral* words and scriptures of the Bible, hidden in unique patterns, arranged in seven realms. These realms reveal a secret pathway to Higher Spiritual Consciousness.

To truly live in our highest potential, it is imperative that we understand how to access our higher spiritual consciousness. To align with our spiritual gifts, we must learn how to spend more time as our higher spiritual selves. To uncover our higher purpose in life we must be able to consistently attain our highest spiritual consciousness.

The concept of "higher spiritual consciousness" generally refers to an elevated or expanded state of awareness and understanding that goes beyond the ordinary aspects of human experience. **Higher Spiritual Consciousness directly correlates with Spiritual Wellness.**

In 'The7Realms, the spiritual consciousness realms exist as *trilateral* (3-part) realms. Many spiritual traditions suggest that higher spiritual consciousness involves a connection to a higher power, whether that is conceived as a divine being, universal energy, or cosmic intelligence.

From a Christian perspective, higher spiritual consciousness includes our ability to experience transcendence to the highest realm of consciousness. I define this highest realm as God-consciousness. 'The7Realms' guides your mindfulness and meditation practice to ultimately accomplish this positive transcendental process.

When we purposefully direct our spiritual energy, in the form of attention (mindfulness) and intention (focused prayer or scriptural meditation), we can use these newly defined realms of spiritual consciousness to ascend to higher consciousness.

In doing so we achieve the transcendental reality of our spiritual being-ness (spiritual consciousness), and we conspire with God to bring our true Self closer to the I AM.

The Organizational Chart of The Seven Trilateral Realms of Spiritual Consciousness

The Seven Trilateral Realms of Spiritual Consciousness (Spiritual Wellness)	The Seven Realms- Highest to Lowest
The Realm of The Trinity - God the Father - God the Son - God the Holy Spirit	**The First Realm** Highest Realm of Spiritual Consciousness and Spiritual Wellness The Realm of Physical Wellness
The Realm of the Fruit of The Spirit - Love - Peace - Joy	**The Second Realm** The Realm of Co-existence in The Spirit
The Realm of Manifestation - Ask - Seek - Knock	**The Third Realm** The Realm of Manifestation from Spiritual Consciousness
The Realm of Consciousness - Mind - Body - Soul	**The Fourth Realm** The Realm of Spiritual Transition from Lower to Higher Consciousness
The Realm of Condemnation - Condemnation - Fear - Worry	**The Fifth Realm** The Initial Realm of Transition into Spiritual Entropy (*The First Realm of Lower Consciousness*)
The Realm of Unforgiveness (*Hatred*) - Unforgiveness - Anger - Doubt	**The Sixth Realm** The Carnal Descent into Lower Consciousness Thoughts, Feeling, and Emotions (*The precursor of physical disease*)
The Realm of Disease Manifestation - Internal Disease - External Disease - Mental/Psychological Disease	**The Seventh Realm** The Lowest Realm of Spiritual Consciousness and Spiritual Unwellness (*The Realm of Physical Disease*)

Understanding the pathway and practice of 'The7Realms' offers the following:

1. Allows you to begin each day in your highest realm of spiritual consciousness.

2. Enables you to recognize where you exist in your realm of spiritual consciousness (your spiritual thoughts, feelings, and emotions) at any given moment.

3. Empowers you with the method to transition from any realm of lower spiritual consciousness (negative thoughts, feelings, and emotions) to the realms of higher spiritual consciousness (positive thoughts, feelings, and emotions) using the newly uncovered trilateral words and scriptures found in 'The7Realms'.

'The7Realms' workbook instructs you on how to use the mindfulness and meditation techniques outlined in this practice to travel along this divinely guided path to attain your higher spiritual consciousness. **This workbook will introduce you to the trilateral words of 'The7Realms' used in the Pyramid of Sovereignty.** The workbook will guide you through the biblical and spiritual definitions of these specific trilateral words and scriptures that make up this newly discovered pathway.

The structure of this divinely guided path is illustrated as a hierarchical pyramid whose realms outline a newly uncovered path through spiritual consciousness. (See Illustration 1).

There are numerous benefits to the Mindfulness and Meditation practice of 'The7Realms':

- Enables you to continually connect with your higher spiritual self, spiritual consciousness, and spiritual wellness.
- Offers an easy-to-follow/step-by-step practice of Christian Mindfulness and Biblical Meditation.
- Introduces you to newly identified trilateral words and scriptures of the Bible and the power they possess when correctly identified with certain realms of consciousness.
- Empowers you to find your authentic vibrational alignment with universal consciousness and Oneness with God.
- Channels your positive spiritual energy and assists you to redirect that spiritual energy to your Higher Self
- Introduces reprogramming of your subconscious mind and subsequently transforms your conscious mind.
- Offers physical restoration through the manifestation of improving spiritual wellness.
- Offers psychological and mental recovery by reprogramming your subconscious mind with a newfound focus on your higher spiritual consciousness

The Pyramidal Structure of The Seven Realms of Spiritual Consciousness:

The Pyramid of Sovereignty

-The Primary Pyramid

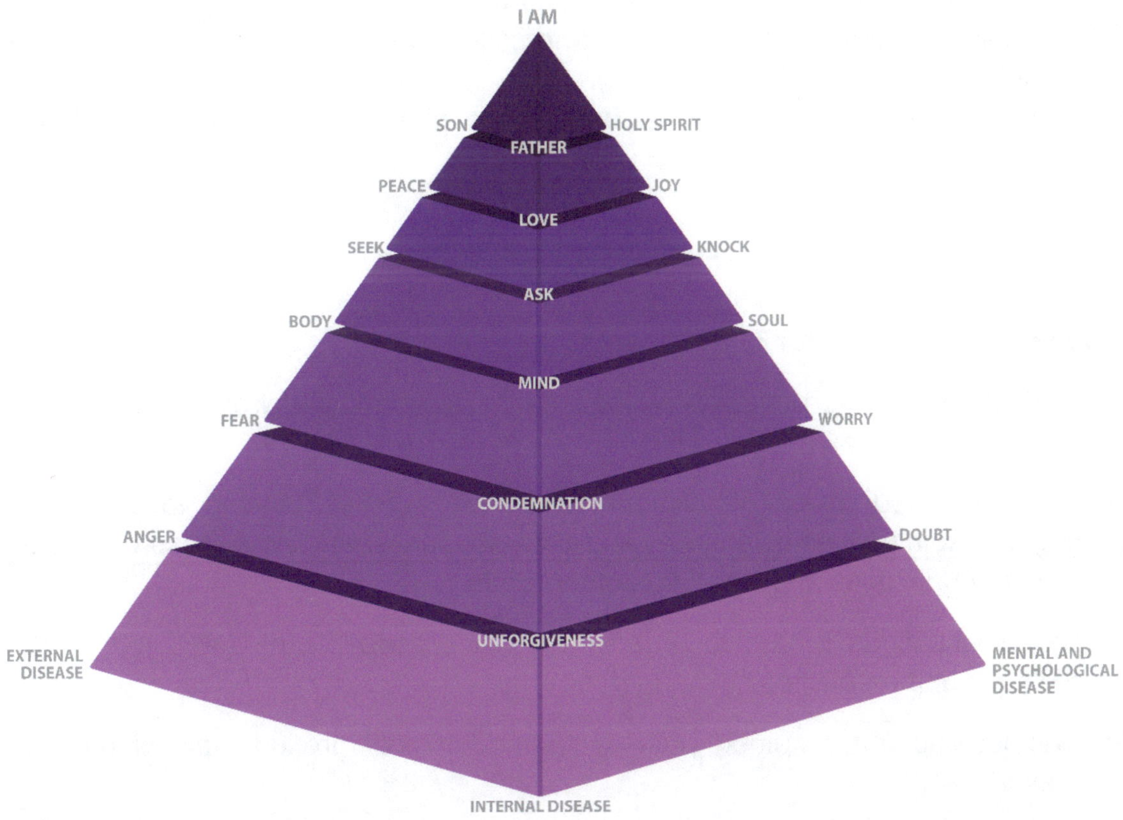
I AM
SON
HOLY SPIRIT
FATHER
PEACE
JOY
LOVE
SEEK
KNOCK
ASK
BODY
SOUL
MIND
FEAR
WORRY
CONDEMNATION
ANGER
DOUBT
UNFORGIVENESS
EXTERNAL DISEASE
MENTAL AND PSYCHOLOGICAL DISEASE
INTERNAL DISEASE

The Pyramid of Sovereignty- Illustration 1

Mastering 'The7Realms':

Once mastered, 'The7Realms' practice will allow you to:

- Transcend to your highest spiritual consciousness at any given moment **(The 1st Realm)**.
- Align your spiritual beingness with your spiritual gift and God's purpose for your life **(The 2nd Realm)**.
- Manifest anything your heart desires by simply asking and believing **(The 3rd Realm)**.
- Consistently dwell in consciousness and mindfulness **(The 4th Realm)**.
- Conquer self-condemnation, fear, and worry **(The 5th Realm)**.
- Overcome unforgiveness, anger and self-doubt and being aware of ever-present spiritual attacks **(The 6th Realm)**.
- Live a long and prosperous life in good physical and mental health **(The 7th Realm)**.

Who is 'The7Realms' for?

Any Christian seeking an easy-to-follow and consistent pathway to mindfulness and meditation.

For everyone, regardless of religious affiliation or belief, looking to understand the concepts of spirituality, universality, and consciousness, and how these concepts might relate to the principles and teachings of the Bible.

Someone who finds it hard to grasp the elusive concepts of traditional practices of mindfulness and meditation.

Anyone looking for a guided path or methodological process for mindfulness and meditation.

For those who require a foundational principle and/or a specific target or goal for meditation.

For any person who finds themselves easily distracted or having a hard time concentrating. (Particularly, someone who struggles with ADHD, OCD, and Neurodivergence and needs a structured outline to grasp the concepts in mindfulness and meditation.)

The Co-creation of 'The7Realms'
The Co-creation of 'The7Realms' describes the historical timeline by which God revealed to me the secrets of The Seven Trilateral Realms of Spiritual Consciousness.

In The Beginning...

As a child, I was fascinated with patterns, shapes, and numbers. My mother noticed, at an early age, my odd attraction for making patterns, shapes, or designs with anything I could get my hands on. I believe I saw the entire world through patterns, shapes, and numbers.

These childhood allures were just a prelude to a lifetime of indulging in and seeking to master my obsession with patterns. I would later come to appreciate this genius as a gift in *pattern recognition*.

The Timeline from 1969 to the Present

1969- The recognition of 'the gift'. My mother first realized my gift of pattern recognition when I was 3-4 years old.

1970-1971- She later noted my ability to perform math problems beyond my age level. When I was 5, she identified my fascination with puzzles.

1972-1987- I spent my entire educational life in Catholic schools from elementary school to high school to college.

1979- In elementary school my gift of pattern recognition allowed me to excel in math and science.

1979-1983- In high school the gift of pattern recognition in math and science began to lend itself to my classes in religion. I began to observe patterns of words in the Bible. I envisioned word patterns that appeared to be grouped into threes. (Examples of these groups of three included words such as *love, peace, and joy*; *ask, seek, and knock*; and *mercy, grace, and hope*.)

1983-1987- In college, I developed a deep desire to reconcile my Christian faith in the principles of the Bible and the Word of God with my evolving understanding of the Laws of Science and Universality.

1986-1987- I took my first class in physical chemistry, otherwise known as quantum mechanics. It was here that God, science, and math, and my gift of pattern recognition came full circle.

1985-2005- I began an intense and passionate self-study of the Bible. I had a deep desire to understand how the Word of God correlated with my life and my special purpose in life. For some reason, I had an urgent need to find my Higher Self. My greater purpose.

1987- I graduated college and entered medical school. My first year in medical school presented me with many personal challenges- including the loss of my grandmother, becoming the caretaker for my 14-year-old brother, and finding out I was about to become a new father.

1987-1991- During medical school and the search for my Higher Self, I began to study the concept of Consciousness. I began to recognize how my studies in the Word of God correlated with Consciousness, particularly Spiritual Consciousness. Subsequently, I discovered how Spiritual Consciousness correlated with Spiritual Wellness.

Lastly, during this medical school period of greater enlightenment, I realized how Spiritual Consciousness and Spiritual Wellness directly correlated with Physical Wellness and Physical Disease.

1991-1995- I decided to organize the word patterns I was noticing in the Bible. I began to put together multiple three-word patterns. I organized these three-words into triangles and called these three-word patterns- *trilateral*. I identified at least 84 *trilateral words/phrases* making up 28 *trilateral patterns*.

1995-2000- I then began to identify *trilateral scriptures* in the Bible. I recognized that many of the most quoted biblical scriptures had a *trilateral cadence*. I also noted that many of these scriptures contained many of my newly discovered trilateral words.

2000- The discovery of 'The7Realms' reveals specific trilateral words and scriptures of the Bible that relate to the Trinity. As such, the Trinity and its three-part essence has become the building block for the mindfulness and meditation practices of 'The7Realms'.

2000-2004- Through divine discernment, I determined that these trilateral words, when placed together in a certain order, correlated with specific levels and realms of consciousness- Spiritual Consciousness.

2005-2010- I began to study the definition and context of each of these trilateral words more closely. I studied the standard definitions of these words as well as the biblical and spiritual definitions of these words.

2010- I recognized that many of these words (in both their standard and biblical/spiritual definitions) could also be expressed as *thoughts, feelings, and emotions*. I surmised that when you put the idea of **thoughts + feelings + emotions** together these concepts equated to a definition for **consciousness**. I decided on an acronym for Thoughts, Feelings, and Emotions= TFEs.

2010-2012- I realized that not only did many of these trilateral words from the Bible represent *thoughts, feelings, and emotions* (TFEs) but in their word essence also appeared to represent a form of energy. This energy could be expressed in the form of **Spiritual Energy, Vibrational Energy, or even Quantum Energy**. I believed that these biblical trilateral words and scriptures also represented the **Energy of Source, of the Oneness of the Universe, the Energy of God**.

2010-2012- I then determined that this spiritual consciousness energy (in the form of the words and scriptures from the Bible (or words as thoughts, feelings, and emotions) could be used as a spiritual pathway, a spiritual corridor, or even a transcendental highway, from the Realms of Lower Spiritual Consciousness (LSC) to the Realms of Higher Spiritual Consciousness (HSC).

2012- I noted that the spiritual pathway could be assessed using one of two ways:

1) The **Practice of Mindfulness**- *Christian, Focused Prayer, or Prayer Mantras.*
2) The **Practice of Meditation**- *Biblical, Transcendental, or Scriptural.*

2012-2018- Through divine ordination I organized these trilateral patterns of biblical words and scriptures into seven realms:

- the seven (7) realms were arranged from Higher to Lower Spiritual Consciousness Realms.
- the seven (7) realms were displayed as three (3)-sided realms (triangles) forming a 3-sided pyramid (tetrahedron) with the Higher Spiritual Realms at the top and the Lower Spiritual Realms at the bottom.
- there were four (4) sets of trilateral realms for each of the seven (7) realms.
- these four (4) sets of trilateral realms were separated into four (4) pyramids.

2018- The four (4) pyramids were as follows:

- The **Pyramid of Sovereignty**
- The **Pyramid of Restoration**
- The **Pyramid of Salvation**
- The **Pyramid of Truth**

And thus, **The Seven Trilateral Realms of Spiritual Consciousness** was born- aka 'The7Realms'.

2018-2020- I then noted that each of the seven realms and four pyramids intersected at their perspective realms of spiritual consciousness to form a multi-dimensional realm. Each multidimensional realm formulated a 12-pointed star dodecagram (created by the overlapping of the four trilateral realms of each of the four pyramids). I came to understand that these multidimensional realms helped to explain the universality of the spiritual consciousness of man.

2020-Present- Each of the pyramids can be used as a backdrop, foundation, structure, or hierarchical pyramidal pathway for the practice of Christian Mindfulness and Biblical Meditation.

These mindfulness and meditation practice/techniques allows you to:

1) Begin your day at your Highest Realm of Spiritual Consciousness.
2) Recognize which Realm of Spiritual Consciousness you exist within in the present moment.
3) Allows you to transcend from Lower Spiritual Consciousness to Higher Spiritual Consciousness using the Mindfulness and Meditation techniques in 'The7Realms'.

As a practicing physician of more than 25 years I also discovered an overarching value of "The7Realms'. The power of 'The7Realms' revealed the secret of how spiritual wellness correlated with spiritual consciousness and that spiritual consciousness and spiritual wellness were interrelated.

The person who existed in positive higher spiritual consciousness or spiritual wellness was much more likely to exist in physical wellness. However, the person who existed in lower spiritual consciousness or spiritual unwellness often existed in physical unwellness or physical disease.

The secrets hidden within 'The7Realms' offered the ability to embrace higher spiritual consciousness and subsequently improve spiritual wellness through the practice of mindfulness and meditation.

The consistent practice of Christian Mindfulness and Biblical Meditation through 'The7Realms' and dwelling in higher spiritual consciousness offers the following benefits:

- The ability to reprogram your subconscious mind.
- The skill to raise your spiritual energy.
- The capability to travel through spiritual consciousness.
- The competency to heal emotional instabilities.
- The capacity to tune into your vibrational alignment.
- The proficiency to balance spiritual energy.
- The information to calm physical disorder and inner turmoil.
- The reduction of stress related disease.
- The power to improve DNA health and telomere health.
- The potential to slow cognitive decline.
- The proficiency to enhance neuroplasticity.

How To Use 'The7Realms' Workbook

In the **Glossary** section of this workbook, you will be introduced to (or reminded of) many of the definitions related to the principles and understanding of consciousness, spirituality, mindfulness, and meditation.

This workbook is divided into **12 Chapters**. Each chapter represents one-week of study. As such, this 12 Chapter workbook can ideally be finished in 12 weeks, but some may choose to take longer. For instance, some people choose to study each chapter over 2 weeks and that's okay. Take your time. Study at your own pace. However, I would recommend that you study the course in the order it is presented in the workbook to get the full effect.

In **Chapters 1-3**, you will be introduced to the principles, themes, and postulates of the newly uncovered secrets of 'The7Realms'.

You will be introduced to 'My Story' and the unique journey I took to get to the discovery of 'The7Realms'.

You will learn about *trilateral words and scriptures*. What they are and how they are used in 'The7Realms'. You will come to understand how these words can guide your present Thoughts, Feelings, and Emotions (TFEs) through specific Realms of Spiritual Consciousness.

Next in **Chapters 4-10**, you will learn the individual principles taught in each of The Seven Realms. Each chapter will review one of The Seven Realms. In each chapter you will be introduced to the standard definition as well as the biblical/spiritual definition of each trilateral word presented in each realm.

Each of these chapters will also contain an **Exercise in Mindfulness and Meditation Practice** and study questions that you are to complete at the end of the chapter.

And finally, in **Chapters 11 and 12**, you will be introduced to the formal meditation process used in 'The7Realms'.

Mastering this formal meditation process can be used daily to allow you to transcend to specific realms of Higher Spiritual Consciousness.

It is recommended that you **start each chapter on Sunday (as Day 1)**. The first day requires the longest amount of time to read the chapter, practice the mindfulness and meditation exercise, and answer the question for Day 1.

After every chapter you will be asked to ponder one question each day (a total of 7 questions each week). Additionally, you will be asked to practice the corresponding **Exercise in Mindfulness and Meditation Practice** each day after answering the question for that day.

Most of these questions are open-ended and will use words like "Contemplate" or "Consider". These questions are intended to elicit an individualized thought process from the reader, participant, or student.

At the end of the 12 weeks (or however long you choose to take in completing this course), it is expected that you will have expanded your knowledge and understanding regarding the principles and secrets hidden in 'The7Realms'.

It is anticipated that after these 12 weeks you would be able to incorporate part, or all, of these techniques into your daily practice of mindfulness and meditation.

In addition, the new concepts, definitions, and postulates outlined are designed to cause you to rethink how you see consciousness. The mindfulness and meditation practices of 'The7Realms' allow for a restructuring of your thoughts and reprogramming your subconscious mind (as it relates to these special biblical words and scriptures).

Next, this transformation will help to grow your time spent in positive Thoughts, Feelings, and Emotions (TFEs) to extend your presence in conscious thought (mindfulness) and thereby improve your ability to transition to higher consciousness (meditation).

Lastly, it is anticipated that over time you will come to slowly appreciate that this continued practice of mindfulness and meditation through 'The7Realms' has slowly, but fully, transformed your conscious mind to a perpetual state of Higher Spiritual Consciousness.

Glossary- Contextual Definition for 'The7Realms'

Attention refers to focusing on or observing something. Attention is the cognitive process that involves observing or becoming aware of something (Mindfulness). In a spiritual or contemplative context, the concept of "attention" often refers to a focused and mindful awareness of the present moment, one's thoughts, emotions, and the surrounding environment.

Biblical Meditation is a practice that involves reflecting upon and contemplating the teachings and messages of the Bible. Biblical meditation is often seen as a form of prayer and a way of deepening one's relationship with God.

Christian Mindfulness is a spiritual practice that involves being present in the moment and cultivating a deep sense of awareness of God's presence in our lives. Through prayer, meditation, and other spiritual practices, we can learn to quiet our minds and connect with God on a deeper level, experiencing a sense of inner peace and contentment that transcends our circumstances.

Consciousness is an abstract and elusive phenomenon that refers to our awareness of ourselves and the world around us. Metaphysical perspectives on consciousness often involve the idea that consciousness is not just a product of the brain but is also a fundamental aspect of the universe. From this perspective, there are various levels of consciousness, each corresponding to distinct levels of reality or dimensions of existence.

Dodecagram: In geometry a dodecagram is a 12-pointed star polygon or compound with 12 vertices. This dodecagram polygon can be made from 4 symmetrical triangles. The spiritual meaning of the 12-pointed star is an ancient symbol meaning divine harmony and integrity, creation, and balance.

Focused Prayer and Focused Prayer Meditation the practice involves taking a passage of scripture, reading it slowly and carefully, and then spending time contemplating its meaning and relevance to one's life.

Higher Spiritual Consciousness (HSC): The concept of "higher spiritual consciousness" generally refers to an elevated or expanded state of awareness and understanding that goes beyond the ordinary or mundane aspects of human experience. Many spiritual traditions suggest that higher spiritual consciousness involves a connection to a higher power, whether that is conceived as a divine being, universal energy, or cosmic intelligence. From a Christian perspective, it includes our ability to experience awe, wonder, and transcendence, and it is often considered to be the highest level of consciousness. 'The7Realms' guides your mindfulness and meditation practice to accomplish this positive transcendental process. These newly defined realms of spiritual consciousness are based on the experience that when we purposefully direct our spiritual energy, in the form of attention (focused prayer) and intention (scriptural meditation), we can ascend to higher consciousness. In doing so we achieve the transcendental reality of our spiritual being-ness (spiritual consciousness), and we conspire with God to bring our true Self closer to the I AM.

Intention or Targeted Spiritual Intention (TSI): A purpose; goal; target; intent. A concept considered as the product of attention. Intention is usually directed to an object of need, expectation, or desire. In spirituality, intention refers to the purposeful and conscious direction of one's thoughts, actions, and energy toward a specific goal, purpose, or desired outcome. It involves the clarity of purpose and the commitment to align one's actions with higher values or spiritual principles.

Lower Spiritual Consciousness (LSC): The term "lower spiritual consciousness" is not as commonly used as its counterpart, "higher spiritual consciousness." Lower states of consciousness evolve from a negative state of spiritual energy. This negative state equates to spiritual unwellness. Moreover, the subconsciousness of our carnal mind rests in, or sometimes actively pursues, negative, unhealthy thoughts, feelings, and emotions. These destructive thoughts, feelings, and emotions exist in the realms of the lower spiritual consciousness (see "Subconsciousness and the Subconscious") Regrettably, the negative downward force of spiritual unwellness tends to occur subconsciously when left unimpeded, allowing your thoughts to continuously descend into lower consciousness thinking. I call this passive descent to negative spiritual energy and lower consciousness thinking- *spiritual entropy.*

Meditation is often referred to as "pondering" or "reflecting." Meditation is the practice of engaging in a deliberate time and formal process of awareness, or mindfulness. The meditation practice of 'The7Realms' involves contemplation of the divinely ordered *trilateral* words and scriptures arranged in a specifically organized progression. The expectation of this meditation practice is the ability to transition through spiritual consciousness to attain higher spiritual consciousness.

Middle Spiritual Consciousness (MSC): In 'The7Realms' the middle consciousness level is equivalent to the Fourth Realm, also known as the realm of Mind, Body and Soul. The Mind, Body, and Soul Realm exists as a single realm, dedicated as a **transitioning**

realm, for the conscious attention (mindfulness) and conscious intention (meditation) on specific *trilateral* words and scriptures. This realm acts as a spiritual partition between the realms that exist as higher consciousness realms and the ones that exist as lower consciousness realms. In other words, this realm serves as a transition zone for mindfulness and meditation when you are travelling from lower consciousness to higher consciousness.

Mindfulness is the ability to be aware (*awareness*), or focus, at any given moment, on a specific thought, feeling, emotion, or even a word. In the case of 'The7realms', we use trilateral biblical words or scriptures as centering mantras or prayers.

Pattern Recognition is the ability to recognize patterns, regularities, or consistent relationships within data, stimuli, or information. It is a fundamental aspect of human cognition and is also a key concept in various fields, including science, mathematics, religion, logic, critical thinking, and cognitive psychology.

Spiritual Beingness and Beingness: "Beingness" is a term that is often used in philosophy and spirituality to refer to the state or quality of being. It is a concept that delves into the essence of existence and the nature of being alive. It goes beyond mere physical existence and may involve considerations of consciousness, self-awareness, and the subjective experience of being. In various philosophical traditions, discussions about beingness may touch upon questions like the nature of consciousness, the self, and the relationship between the individual and the broader cosmos. It's a concept that invites contemplation and exploration into the deeper dimensions of existence.

Spiritual Consciousness: This level of consciousness is associated with our connection to a higher power or a greater sense of meaning and purpose in life. In 'The7Realms' there is the construct of **Higher, Middle, and Lower Spiritual Consciousness.** (See specific definitions for Higher, Middle, and Lower Spiritual Consciousness in the Glossary)

Spiritual Energy (SEn): The term "spiritual energy" is often used in various spiritual and metaphysical contexts to describe a form of energy that is associated with the non-physical or transcendent aspects of existence. It is seen as an energy that transcends the material world and connects individuals to higher states of consciousness or spiritual dimensions. Spiritual energy can be associated as positive spiritual energy or negative spiritual energy.

Spiritual Entropy (SEt): In a metaphorical sense, the term spiritual entropy is used to describe a state of spiritual disarray, a decline in spiritual well-being, or an increase in negative spiritual influences. It also suggests a loss of coherence, purpose, or positive energy within one's spiritual journey. In 'The7Realms' the term "spiritual entropy" refers to a tendency or measure of disorder, chaos, or spiritual degradation within an individual's spiritual life or the broader spiritual realm.

Scriptural Meditation: It is a way of focusing the mind and spirit on the wisdom and guidance offered by the scriptures. *(See Biblical Meditation)*

Spiritual Realms: the term "spiritual realms" refers to non-physical dimensions or planes of existence that are believed to exist beyond the material world. In 'The7Realms' there are higher and lower spiritual planes or dimensions. These planes may be associated with different levels of consciousness, enlightenment, or vibrational frequencies.

Spiritual Unwellness is the opposite of Spiritual Wellness. It refers to the state of one's lack of spiritual health and well-being. It involves the loss of meaning, purpose, and a sense of connection to something greater than oneself. Spiritual unwellness can also contribute to a greater sense of inner turmoil, unhappiness, and discontentment. Spiritual *un*wellness leads to physical *un*wellness, or physical disease.

Spiritual Wellness refers to the state of one's spiritual health and well-being. It involves finding meaning, purpose, and a sense of connection to something greater than oneself. Spiritual wellness can also contribute to a greater sense of inner peace, happiness, and contentment.

Subconsciousness and the Subconscious: The subconscious refers to the part of the mind that is not in immediate awareness but can influence thoughts, feelings, and behavior. The subconscious mind is thought to contain memories, desires, and information that are not currently in conscious awareness but can still affect a person's actions and thoughts. Unlike the conscious mind, which includes thoughts and feelings of which a person is actively aware, the subconscious operates below the level of conscious awareness.

Tetrahedron: A 3-sided pyramid-in geometry a tetrahedron is also known as a triangular pyramid. It is a polyhedron composed of four triangular faces. The tetrahedron is this simplest all ordinary convex polyhedron and is considered the strongest and most stable polyhedron.

The 4 Pyramids of Spiritual Consciousness and Spiritual Wellness: 'The7Realms' exist across 4 Pyramids. The 4 pyramids are as follows- **The Pyramid of Sovereignty** (the primary foundational pyramid- *the purple pyramid*), **The Pyramid of Restoration** (*the green pyramid*), **The Pyramid of Salvation** (*the red pyramid*), and **The Pyramid of Truth** (*the blue pyramid*). Geometrically these pyramids are called tetrahedrons (or 3-sided pyramids).

The Seven Realms or The Seven Trilateral Realms of Spiritual Consciousness is a spiritual pathway leading to higher consciousness through biblical meditation. 'The7Realms' is the unique discovery of a distinctive correlation between spiritual wellness, spiritual consciousness, and the words of the Bible.

Thoughts, Feelings, and Emotions (TFE's)- Thoughts, feelings, and emotions are interconnected aspects of human experience, but they have distinct characteristics and roles. Thoughts shape feelings and emotions, and they, in turn, influence our behavior. **Thoughts** refer to the cognitive processes and mental activities involving reasoning, perception, memory, and problem-solving. They are often conscious and deliberate, originating from our conscious and subconscious mind. **Feelings** are subjective experiences that arise in response to thoughts, situations, or stimuli. They are often associated with bodily sensations and can be described as pleasant or unpleasant, neutral, or mixed. **Emotions** are intense, relatively brief, and instinctive responses to stimuli, events, or situations. They involve physiological changes, such as increased heart rate or changes in facial expressions. Emotions are often considered more primal and automatic compared to thoughts and feelings.

Trilateral: The definition of trilateral, as an adjective, means shared by or involving three parties. I chose the word *trilateral* to describe the patterns of words and scriptures I uncovered in the Bible. These trilateral patterns and concepts represent the realms within 'The7Realms'. The word trilateral fits with the core basis of my sacred belief in the Trinity. (See Chapter 1.3- The Powerful Discovery of Trilateral Words)

Trilateral Spiritual Realms (TSR): In "The7Realms', I identify seven trilateral realms of spiritual consciousness. I called these seven realms *trilateral* because they contained three interconnected words or scriptures. These realms represent *trilateral concepts* because they evolved from and contain the postulate that specific words of the Bible correlate with certain realms of spiritual consciousness and generate a certain level of energy or power. In 'The7Realms' there are **unidimensional spiritual realms** and **multi-dimensional spiritual realms.**

Trilateral Words and Scriptures (TWS): The Seven Trilateral Realms of Spiritual Consciousness contains 84 trilateral words and scriptures in the Bible that correspond to levels of spiritual consciousness, and subsequently spiritual wellness. (See the definition of Trilateral)

Trinity/The Doctrine of The Trinity- The doctrine of the Trinity is a fundamental concept in Christian theology that attempts to explain the nature of God as three distinct persons in one divine being. It is essential to note that the concept of the Trinity is not explicitly stated in the Bible but is a theological interpretation derived from various biblical passages. The discovery of 'The7Realms' reveals specific trilateral words and scriptures of the Bible that relate to the Trinity. As such, **the Trinity and its three-part essence has become the building block for the mindfulness and meditation practices of 'The7Realms'.**

Universal Consciousness: This level of consciousness is associated with the idea that all things in the universe are interconnected and part of a larger, unified consciousness. It includes the idea that consciousness exists beyond the physical body and is a fundamental aspect of the universe itself.

Vibrational Alignment (VAI) and Spiritual Vibrational Alignment (SVA) refer to the idea that an individual can attune or align their personal energy with higher, more positive, or harmonious frequencies.

Vibrational Energy (VE) and Vibrational Energy Frequencies (VEF) refers to the quantum measurement used for quantifying energy. In various spiritual and metaphysical contexts, where it may be associated with the idea that everything in the universe is in a state of vibration, and different frequencies correspond to different states of being.

'The7Realms'
The Workbook

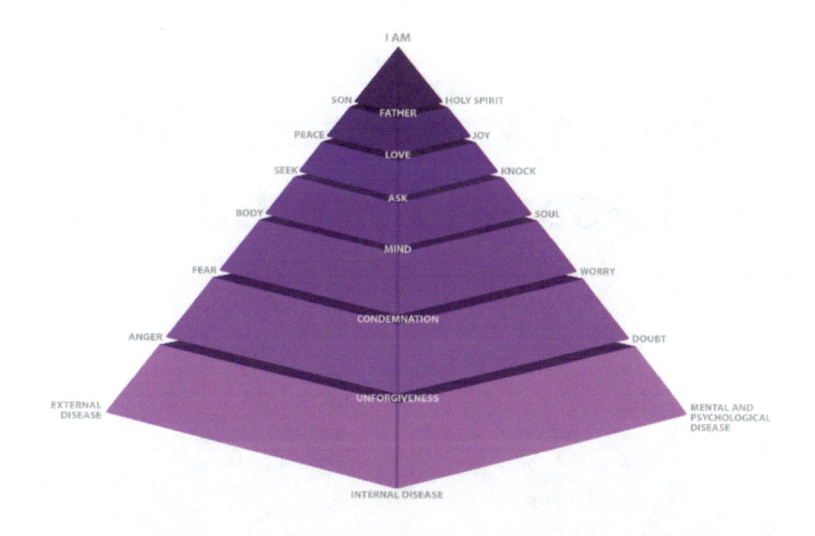

The Pyramid of Sovereignty

(The Primary Pyramid)

Week 1/Lesson 1: Introduction- Spiritual Consciousness and Spiritual Energy

Lesson 1: Introduction

1.1- The Divine Right of Spiritual Wellness

1.2- My Story- God, Science, and Math

1.3- The Powerful Discovery of Trilateral Words and Scriptures

1.4- Christian Mindfulness and Biblical Meditation

1.5- Definition of Consciousness, Spiritual Consciousness, and Spiritual Wellness

1.6- Spiritual Energy and Consciousness Travel

1.7- The Energy of Consciousness

1.8- The Energy/Power of the Visualized, the Heard, and the Spoken Word

1.9- Thoughts, Feelings, and Emotions (TFEs)

1.10- Prayer and Meditation Evoke Higher Spiritual Energy

Questions for Week 1/Lesson 1

1.1- The Divine Right of Spiritual Wellness

An Infinite Being

You are a finite and an infinite being. Your life is a finite and an infinite time continuum of God's choosing. As a spiritual being having a human experience, your humanness makes you finite.

Before your finite existence came into human beingness, your spirit was with God, which I interpret as *pre-finite*. And I believe, that at the time of your death, your departure from your human beingness, you will return to your spiritual beingness, and you will spend your eternal existence with God, thereby, making you infinite.

While some may interpret my definitions of finite, pre-finite, and infinite as a proclamation of self-deity, let me assure you that I am not so presumptuous, as to define my human or spiritual existence in any equivalent state of Gods existence. As I believe God to be the only true eternal, omnipotent, and omnipresent deity.

Whether I am in my finite or infinite state, my spiritual being is always *of* God, *from* God, and *in* God.

Therefore, as a finite, pre-finite, and infinite being, life and death are equal and opposing existences of the same time continuum. The beginning and the end of the self-same Oneness known as, the "I AM".

"And the Lord God formed man of the dust of the ground and breathed into his nostrils the breath of life; and man became a living being." **{Genesis 2:7-NKJV}**

The Divine Right of Spiritual Wellness

We are created by the Creator with the divine right of wellness. The God of the universe, the Source, and the Oneness of man breathed life into His creation he called man and woman.

Thus, before we were conceived into this time continuum of life in human form, we were perfect spiritual-beings, in a perfect state of spiritual wellness, at the highest level of spiritual consciousness and in the existence of God's omnipresence.

As spiritual beings having a human experience, we are all perfect beings. As spiritual beings, made as human beings, we exist within the perfect realm of spiritual wellness.

This perfect realm of spiritual wellness exists at the highest level of spiritual consciousness and spiritual enlightenment.

I believe this realm is in concordance with the perfect spiritual realm known as "The Trinity"- God the Father, God the Son, and God the Holy Spirit.

1.2- My Story- God, Science, and Math

Patterns, Shapes, and Numbers

As a child, I was fascinated with patterns, shapes, and numbers. My mother noticed, as early as three years of age, my odd attraction to making patterns, shapes, or designs with anything I could get my hands on. Sometimes, while playing outside with the other kids, I would stop and stoop down to the ground and begin to arrange random sticks or rocks into different patterns or designs.

My mother would recall me pointing out different patterns everywhere I would go. I would become excited about the patterns of the clouds in the sky, trees in the park, bricks on a building, and even cans in the grocery store.

Strangely, some of the most intriguing patterns for me were the ones I observed on linoleum floors in the kitchens of the 1970s. I remember staring at the linoleum trying to visualize how all the patterns fit together. I found this same fascination with the patterns of mosaic tiles found in many bathrooms of the same era. (This fascination would often get me in trouble as my mother would become frustrated with the amount of time I would spend in bathrooms whenever and wherever I encountered this tile.)

I would also spend hours playing with *Legos* and *Lincoln Logs.* I would play with these toys for hours trying to uncover the different buildings, shapes, and arrangements I could create.

As I got older, I encountered the magic of puzzles. I loved how the oddly shaped pieces could be fitted together to form a hidden picture. Unfolding the hidden picture from the jumbled pieces was intoxicating for me.

I would reportedly become so enthralled while working on a puzzle, my mother complained that I would often ignore her when she called me or tried to get my attention. She would later explain that while working on a puzzle, it was as if I had entered a trance-like state.

Despite this occasional disregard for my mother's voice, she always indulged my creativity. I would often hear her say to other people, "I think he is going to be an architectural engineer." While I was not sure what an architectural engineer was, I assumed it had something to do with building blocks and puzzles.

Next came my fascination with numbers and math. By age 4-5, I could already do simple math problems. I would ask my mother to buy me math books instead of coloring books. As a child, I felt as if uncovering the answers to math problems was magical.

Math books were just like puzzles to me. I especially liked that math always had a definitive answer. I was delighted to finish one book and solve all the problems, just so I could get a new math book with new problems to solve.

I believe I saw the entire world through patterns, shapes, and numbers. These childhood allures were just a prelude to a lifetime of indulging in and seeking to master my obsession with patterns. I would later come to appreciate this genius as a gift in *pattern recognition.*

Math, Science, and Religion

I continued my fascination with patterns and numbers in elementary and high school. I was a 'natural' in math and continuously excelled in it. In part, I think, because I could always find a specific pattern to reach a finite and definitive answer to any problem. Every number had a discrete measure. The unfolding of a math answer was like magic to me. Math spoke to me- it was like a language. I would later come to learn that math was considered *the language of God.*

As my understanding of more complex math problems expanded, I became aware of the different patterns, equations or algorithms that were possible to get to a precise answer. In high school, I was mesmerized with the different mathematical computations and calculations, all of which could be used to derive at a particular resolution.

I also noticed similar patterns in the discipline of science, especially when math was essential to explain the principle of scientific rule or law. The patterns between math and science became most obvious to me in the science of chemistry. I likewise excelled in chemistry, in large part because of its marriage to math.

My combined obsessions with numbers, patterns, math, and science persisted throughout my high school years. It was here that I began to develop the belief that everything in life had a pattern or a formula or a specific order. I believed that if I could find the pattern in a thing, I could answer any question in the world or unlock any secret of the universe.

During my junior year in high school, I decided I wanted to become a physician. The dream of going to medical school and studying to become a physician felt like the perfect transition to apply my love for both science and math. I believed that through the study of medicine I would discover the secrets of the mind, body, and soul, and combine this knowledge with my passion for visualizing patterns and algorithms to heal the world.

My Parochial School Upbringing

It is worth noting that I spent the entirety of my school years in religious institutions. I went to Catholic schools throughout my elementary, high school, and college years.

As I attended parochial schools, religion was a required course each year. During my transitioned from high school to college, I started to recognize, what I interpreted to be, unique numerical patterns hidden in specific words and scriptures of the Bible. These words seem to appear in patterns of three. These findings fueled my desire to explore how detecting these patterns, in the words and scriptures, might reveal a hidden secret or unlock a yet undetermined mystery in the Bible.

I started this exploration by identifying any patterns of the most commonly used words in the Bible. I then began to research the definition and interpretation of these words. I sought to ascertain if my newly perceived recognition of such patterns, related to any of these commonly used words, and if these patterns were consistent. I felt that if I could determine a connection to the meaning, or concept, of these most used words, and establish a relationship to the newly revealed patterns, then I might be able to uncover a hidden meaning or purpose for these unique words and patterns.

In college however, my interest in these numerical patterns turned into an obsession. This obsession began with my introduction to a required pre-med college course which combined the study of both math and science (physics and chemistry) called physical chemistry. Better known as *quantum mechanics or quantum physics*. It was here that everything changed. Unlocking the principles taught in physical chemistry put into context almost every other discipline I had studied thus far, including religion. It was here that my interpretation of the universe and its intrinsic secrets gradually began to unfold. This new preoccupation came together in my mind as 'God, Science, and Math', and became my newfound gateway to the path of spiritual consciousness.

A Tumultuous Time

Being schooled in a religious environment for the entirety of my early educational years undoubtedly affected my conscious and subconscious beliefs surrounding God and Christianity. I am also certain this spiritual upbringing directed my thoughts and actions throughout the course of my life. I was always intrigued by the biblical ideas and teachings of Jesus Christ. My devotion to biblical and scriptural theories grew progressively in college as I read the Bible from front to back, apart from Revelation.

I am deeply indebted and grateful to this enduring exposure to the Christian faith. Despite this experience I make no claims of being a theologian, only a student of the Bible. And while I was not completely aware of how this ongoing background and subliminal messaging permeated the entirety of my spirit, and my soul man, I had always known it was a part of me.

My first year in medical school was very tumultuous. Two months into medical school my beloved grandmother would succumb to cancer. I became the caregiver for my 14-year-old brother. And as if that were not enough, I found out my girlfriend of two years was pregnant with our first child. All this while withstanding the crushing weight of study required of a first-year medical student.

What to do? How was I going to survive it all?

Enter 'The Word of God'.

Because of this forced maturation process, I was compelled to take a deeper look into my spiritual countenance. I now desired, more than ever before, to fully embrace the words that I had studied my entire life. The words of the Bible. My expectation was that they could give me the guidance and comfort I so desperately needed and help me endure my ever-growing struggles.

I sought to better understand God's purpose for my life. I needed to find out what He wanted me to do. I was anxious to achieve God-consciousness, so that I could hear His answers more clearly. My hope was achieving higher consciousness would clarify the path He desired for my life. I wished for some expedient answers to all life questions as things seemed to be moving pretty fast.

Of course, this was easier said than done. Up to this time I had felt that "I" was in control of everything I had accomplished in my life. I believed that I was the sole reason I had made it this far. I thought God was only there, on the sidelines, to help if I needed Him to "make crooked paths straight", or to perform the occasional necessary miracle.

I had not yet come to the realization that everything that I had done, and everything I would do, was orchestrated by God. And that my primary role, in this life of human beingness, was to discover God's will and purpose for my life, and to follow Him.

Lucky for me, during this very turbulent time, God would open my eyes and make it abundantly clear that it had been Him all along. And that the secret was there all along as well, hidden in plain sight, right in front of me, in the words I has studied my entire life- the Words of the Bible.

1.3- The Powerful Discovery of Trilateral Words and Scriptures

My Journey to Spiritual Consciousness

My sacred search began more than 30 years ago, through my own journey for life's greater meaning. This search began with my passionate self-study of the Bible.

As a practicing physician, who spent his entire pre-medicine educational years, from elementary school to college, in Catholic institutions, I was always surreptitiously balancing the rules of science with the teachings of the Gospel of Christ Jesus.

I had a deep longing to favorably reconcile the coexistence of the Principles of Science and Universality, Spirituality, and Christianity.

Moreover, I felt that understanding the principles behind these varied ideologies would help me to discover my higher purpose. My special life's purpose.

So, I begin by seeking to better comprehend the doctrine of the Bible- The Word of God. My journey led me to a daily practice of mindfulness and meditation.

This practice uncovered a secret path, hidden in the passages of the Bible. The secret path was revealed to me through my divine gift of pattern recognition. And it was through this gift that I discovered the doctrines of **The Seven Realms of Spiritual Consciousness** (aka 'The7Realms').

As a result, 'The7Realms' became the foundation of my Christian Mindfulness and Biblical Meditation practice that ultimately changed my life forever.

The Trilateral Words of The Bible

Depending on which Bible you reference, there are over 770000 words in the Bible, approximately 31000 scriptures, and more than 1100 chapters.

Many of the words in the Bible are used repeatedly to emphasize important and similar concepts and precepts of the Bible.

Over the last 30 years I have studied some of the most used words in the Bible. As I studied these words, many of these commonly used words begin to formulate fascinating patterns.

Through my divine gift of pattern recognition, I was able to arrange many of these words into 3-part word patterns. The 3-part word patterns were based on the word's relation to a given biblical principle, truth, concept, or precept.

Over time it began to appear that these 3-word patterns formulated concepts in consciousness, in particular, spiritual consciousness.

In addition, many of these 3-word patterns appeared to represent spiritual consciousness at different realms, from the spectrum of lower spiritual consciousness to higher spiritual consciousness. I named these realms *trilateral*, based on their 3-word composition.

For me, the trilateral word concept was related to the concept of the Trinity. As such, **the Trinity and its three-part essence has become the building block for the mindfulness and meditation practices of 'The7Realms'.**

The Power of the Trilateral Word

In addition to representing The Trinity in the Bible, the number three represents divinity, completeness, and wholeness. The number three also symbolizes harmony, wisdom and understanding. In 'The7Realms' the power of trilateral words is related to the power of The Trinity and the power of the number three.

When connected by the level of their energy these 3-word patterns formed a hierarchical pyramid which when arranged in the proper alignment would allow you to travel from the lowest realms of spiritual consciousness to the highest realms of spiritual consciousness.

As I studied these words more closely, I recognized that each of these words had a power or an energy within the word's meaning in the Bible. The meaning or context of the word in the scripture seemed to frequently describe an energy- such as love, peace, and joy.

When put together in the 3-part patterns the concept or precept of these word patterns existed within their own realm of energy.

In addition, I discovered that there were scriptures in the Bible which also had a 3-part cadence, or *trilateral cadence*. This means you could read or recite the scripture in a 3-part rhythm. Once again, I relate the discovery of trilateral cadences to The Trinity.

When these scriptures were spoken, it was clear that the sound energy, or the vibratory energy, from the speaker's voice resonated power.

When scriptures are written or spoken in a trilateral cadence they represent powerful energy released into one's subconscious mind and subsequently into the universal consciousness.

Moreover, when these words were read or studied or meditated on, these scriptures would also resonate with powerful inner energy for the reader, student, or meditator.

While studying these trilateral scriptures it also became evident that these scriptures contained many of the trilateral words, and when the trilateral words were in the trilateral scriptures, they offered a synergistic energy as well. As such, these trilateral words and trilateral scriptures were therefore often associated with the same trilateral realms.

I became more intrigued than ever. Were these combinations of trilateral words and trilateral scriptures trying to tell me something?

Mindfulness and Meditation in 'The7Realms'

By organizing these patterns, I began to formulate a process by which I was able to **practice mindfulness** (Christian Mindfulness) using any one of these trilateral words or trilateral scriptures. This practice of mindfulness allowed me to become aware (in the present moment) of the specific realm of spiritual consciousness I existed within at that moment.

Secondly, by using the trilateral scriptures, I was able to put together **a practice of meditation** (Biblical Meditation) which allowed me to travel from any realm of lower spiritual consciousness (negative thoughts, feelings, or emotions) to any realm of higher spiritual consciousness (positive thoughts, feelings, or emotions) through the process of meditation on these appropriately arranged trilateral words or trilateral scriptures.

As such, **The Seven Trilateral Realms of Spiritual Consciousness** aka 'The7Realms' was born.

In Conclusion: Spiritual Consciousness and Spiritual Wellness

'The7Realms' outlines a newly discovered pathway through a unique set of spiritual realms of consciousness.

The newly discovered path is traversed by way of a mindfulness and meditation practice using traditional Christian principles and teachings.

This mindfulness and meditation practice allows you to, both easily and consistently, transcend to higher spiritual consciousness and subsequently spiritual wellness.

I uncovered the secret pathway of 'The7Realms' hidden in plain sight throughout some of the most commonly recounted words and scriptures of the Bible.

This compelling discovery was intrinsically woven into the prose tapestry of the Bible and has been unveiled by me for the world to appreciate.

Spiritual consciousness and spiritual wellness are parallel existences within the spheres of conscious thought. Spiritual wellness exists in higher spiritual consciousness, whereas spiritual unwellness exists in lower spiritual consciousness.

As a physician I came to realize that spiritual wellness equates to physical wellness. As such, when you seek to attain higher spiritual consciousness you subsequently also achieve physical wellness. And thus began my divine transformation from a physician who focuses on treating the physical man only, to a more conscious physician who also focuses on acknowledging and healing the spiritual man as well.

1.4 -Christian Mindfulness and Biblical Meditation

Christian Mindfulness

Christian Mindfulness is a spiritual practice that involves being present in the moment and cultivating a deep sense of awareness of God's presence in our lives.

Through prayer, meditation, and other spiritual practices, we can learn to quiet our minds and connect with God on a deeper level, experiencing a sense of inner peace and contentment that transcends our circumstances.

By focusing on the present moment, we can develop a greater appreciation for the beauty and wonder of God's creation and become more attuned to His guidance and direction.

Christian mindfulness is not about emptying our minds or escaping from reality, but rather about learning to be fully present in each moment, trusting in God's goodness and grace, and finding joy and meaning in the journey of life.

Biblical Meditation

Biblical Meditation is a practice that involves reflecting upon and contemplating the teachings and messages of the Bible. Biblical meditation is often seen as a form of prayer and a way of deepening one's relationship with God.

In the Bible, meditation is often referred to as "pondering" or "reflecting." The practice involves taking a passage of scripture, reading it slowly and carefully, and then spending time contemplating its meaning and relevance to one's life.

This may involve asking questions, seeking deeper understanding, and praying for insight and guidance.

Overall, biblical meditation is a way of connecting with God and seeking greater understanding and wisdom through the study and contemplation of scripture.

1.5-Definition of Consciousness, Spiritual Consciousness, and Spiritual Wellness

Consciousness

Consciousness is a complex and often elusive concept that can be understood and defined in different ways, depending on the context in which it is discussed. *At its core, consciousness refers to the state or quality of being aware of and able to think and perceive one's thoughts, surroundings, and experiences.*

*** Thoughts + Feelings + Emotions (Mind) = Consciousness ***

Consciousness involves being aware of both the external world (sensory perception) and the internal world (spiritual intuition). It's the state of knowing that you exist and are experiencing something. A significant aspect of consciousness is self-awareness, which is the ability to reflect upon one's own thoughts, feelings, and emotions and to have a sense of identity and selfhood (mindfulness).

Spiritual Consciousness

Spiritual consciousness can refer to a state of awareness or understanding that goes beyond the physical realm and connects individuals to a higher or transcendent reality.

This state of consciousness is often associated with spiritual or religious experiences, such as feeling a sense of oneness with the universe, experiencing a deep inner peace or joy, spiritual wellness or feeling a connection to a divine or spiritual force.

*** Thoughts + Feelings + Emotions (Mind) (Spirit) = Spiritual Consciousness ***

Spiritual consciousness may involve a shift in perception or perspective that allows individuals to see beyond their ego and identify with a larger sense of purpose or meaning in life. This shift can lead to a greater sense of empathy, compassion, and understanding for others, as well as a greater sense of connection to nature and the world around us.

Some practices that can help cultivate spiritual consciousness include meditation, prayer, mindfulness, and reflection on spiritual teachings or texts.

Spiritual Wellness

Spiritual wellness refers to the state of one's spiritual health and well-being. It involves finding meaning, purpose, and a sense of connection to something greater than oneself.

Higher Spiritual Consciousness = Spiritual Wellness

Spiritual wellness encompasses various aspects, including beliefs, values, ethics, principles, and the exploration of existential questions about life, death, and the nature of reality.

Spiritual wellness can be influenced by religious, philosophical, or metaphysical beliefs. It goes beyond religious affiliations and encompasses a broader sense of spirituality that is unique to everyone.

Some people find spiritual wellness through organized religion, while others may explore spirituality through personal introspection.

Spiritual Consciousness and Spiritual Wellness

In 'The7Realms' spiritual consciousness and spiritual wellness are parallel existences within the spheres of conscious thought.

Sphere of Conscious Thought ⇔ Spiritual Consciousness ⇔ Spiritual Wellness

Spiritual wellness exists in higher spiritual consciousness, whereas spiritual unwellness exists in lower spiritual consciousness.

Lower Spiritual Consciousness = Spiritual Unwellness

Lower spiritual consciousness exists predominately as the subconscious, and often manifests as negative thoughts, feelings, and emotions.

Your Spiritual Beingness

In 'The7realms', the conscious and the subconscious mind coexist as your spiritual beingness.

*** The Conscious Mind + The Subconscious Mind = Spiritual Beingness ***

The subconscious mind is an ever-evolving product of your conscious thoughts, feelings, and emotions. It is constantly nurtured by the ever-present internal and external stimuli of the world.

Depending on the quality and nature of input into your subconscious mind, it Is far too easy for the subconscious mind to grow more in its negative experiences over its positive ones.

The negative energy imprint from exposure to fear and anxiety may override the more positive experience to love and peace.

The lower vibrational frequency of negative spiritual energy is easier to connect with than the higher frequency needed to resonate with higher spiritual energy.

*** Lower Vibrational Frequency = Negative Spiritual Energy ***

(Lower Vibrational Frequency is easier to connect because it requires less energy.)

In the early stages of exposure (even childhood), the predominant input into the subconscious mind originates from the conscious mind and conscious experiences. Often the negative experiences in early childhood leave a much more powerful negative imprint on our subconscious mind than the positive experiences leave a positive imprint.

As the subconscious grows, it takes on a 'mind of its own' and begins to function autonomously and independently of its conscious counterpart. It is this autonomous functioning of the subconscious mind that can later lead to the inappropriate development of the carnal mind and neglected suppression of inner child wounds.

The Carnal Mind

The carnal mind is a mind that is focused on the self and things. It is sometimes referred to as *the egoic mind*.

Being carnally minded is the opposite of being spiritual minded. It is in direct opposition to being God conscious.

"For to be carnally minded is death but to be spiritually minded is life and peace." **Romans 8:6**

Subconsciously the carnal mind rests in, or sometimes actively pursues, negative and unhealthy thoughts. These destructive subconscious thoughts exist in the realms of the lower spiritual consciousness.

Often, these negative thoughts are the by-products of neglect, or misdirected focus, on negative *spiritual energy*.

The Subconscious Controls

In the end, the subconscious mind controls over 95 percent of our waking thoughts, feelings, and emotions. Many of these subconscious thoughts can default to more negative, or unwell, thoughts.

Higher Vibrational Frequency = Positive Spiritual Energy

To rise above our predominantly subconscious existence, we must actively engage conscious awareness (mindfulness). We must actively pursue higher consciousness thought (meditation).

Imagine, if we could redirect even a small percentage of the time and energy spent in subconsciously unwell thoughts, and refocus that energy onto our higher consciousness, we would make incredible inroads into our spiritual well-beingness.

Spiritual Consciousness and Spiritual Wellness Affects Physical Disease

The complex relationship between spiritual consciousness and physical health is a subject that transcends the boundaries of conventional medicine and delves into the realm of holistic well-being.

Spiritual consciousness, often rooted in a sense of purpose, connection to a higher power, or inner self-awareness, can significantly influence the development and progression of physical diseases.

While the connection between spiritual consciousness and physical health is complicated, its importance underscores the need for addressing the holistic well-being of individuals, recognizing that spiritual wellness can play a pivotal role in promoting and sustaining physical health.

Spiritual Consciousness and Spiritual Wellness Affects Mental and Psychological Diseases

The relationship between spiritual consciousness and mental well-being is complex and can significantly influence mental and psychological health.

Spiritual wellness, rooted in a deep connection to one's purpose, values, or a higher power, holds the potential to influence the development and management of mental and psychological diseases.

Individuals with a strong spiritual foundation often report enhanced emotional resilience and coping mechanisms, protecting against the stresses that can contribute to conditions like anxiety and depression.

Practices such as meditation, prayer, or contemplation, central to spiritual consciousness, have demonstrated benefits in reducing symptoms of various mental health disorders. Furthermore, a sense of spiritual meaning and purpose in life can act as a protective factor, offering individuals a framework to navigate experiential challenges and find solace in times of emotional distress.

1.6-Spiritual Energy and Consciousness Travel

Spiritual Energy

Spiritual energy is the energy your conscious mind uses to navigate your thoughts, feelings, and emotions through your spiritual beingness (consciousness).

Thoughts + Emotions + Feelings + Spiritual Consciousness = Spiritual Energy

Each realm in 'The7Realms' represents a different level of spiritual energy.

Negative spiritual energy leads to lower consciousness thoughts whereas positive spiritual energy produces higher consciousness thoughts.

Negative Spiritual Energy = Lower Consciousness Thoughts (often subconscious)

Positive Spiritual Energy = Higher Consciousness Thoughts (often conscious)

The subconscious and unconscious internal dialogue of lower consciousness thoughts *coerces* you into a negative state of spiritual beingness. Your spiritual beingness affects your physical beingness and thus your state of wellness.

This spiritual coercion can unintentionally cause you to shift from higher spiritual consciousness (spiritual wellness) to lower spiritual consciousness (spiritual unwellness). 'The7Realms' teaches you how to overcome this coercion through its unique practices of mindfulness and meditation using trilateral words and scriptures from the Bible.

Consciousness Travel

Consequently, we may subconsciously shift from a state of spiritual wellness to a state of spiritual unwellness in a matter of seconds.

Spiritual Wellness ⇔ Spiritual Unwellness (subconsciously)

We can go from a feeling of peace in one moment to thoughts of worry in the next, by submissively allowing a negative subconscious shift in spiritual energy or focus. Lower spiritual consciousness evolves from a state of negative spiritual energy. This negative state equates to spiritual unwellness.

'The7Realms' teaches you how to move out of this state of lower consciousness to one of higher consciousness by directing an intentional focus on positive spiritual energy by simply using the appropriate aligned trilateral words.

Spiritual Entropy

Let's examine spiritual unwellness first. Regrettably, the negative downward force of spiritual unwellness tends to occur subconsciously and is frequently left unimpeded.

Higher Consciousness = Spiritual Wellness

⬇

Spiritual Entropy

(subconscious negative thoughts)

⬇

Lower Consciousness = Spiritual Unwellness

Being unaware of this subconscious negative influence allows your thoughts to continually descend into lower consciousness thinking. I call this ongoing passive descent to negative spiritual energy and lower consciousness thinking- *spiritual entropy*.

Inner Dialogue of the Carnal Mind

The evolution of these negative thoughts and perceptions grows from the improper attention placed on the subconscious and unconscious inner dialogue of the carnal man and seed the deepest recesses of the carnal mind.

To overcome the subconscious apathy created by this inner dialogue, you must reverse the conversation. You must apply the appropriate positive spiritual *energy* to transcend the spiritual *entropy* and move to a state of higher spiritual consciousness and subsequently spiritual wellness.

Understanding which realm your thoughts exist within- at any given moment- empowers you to understand *where and how* you must direct your spiritual energy to travel to higher consciousness. Understanding the organization of trilateral words and scriptures taught in the mindfulness and meditation practice of 'The7Realms' enables you to overcome spiritual entropy. (See Illustration 1)

Higher versus Lower Spiritual Consciousness in 'The7Realms'

Higher Spiritual Consciousness
[Positive Spiritual Energy]
(The Spirit Mind)

The 7 Realms of Spiritual Consciousness

'I AM'

The Trinity

The Fruit of the Spirit

The Realm of Manifestation

The Realm Mind, Body, and Soul

The Realm of Condemnation, Fear, and Worry

The Realm of Hatred (Self- Hatred), Anger, and Doubt

The Realm of Disease Manifestation- Internal, External and Mental Disease

Lower Spiritual Consciousness

[Negative Spiritual Energy]

(The Carnal Mind)

(Illustration 1- The Seven Realms of Spiritual Consciousness)

1.7-The Energy of Consciousness

Definition of Energy

Energy can be defined as the inherent capacity or potential within a system to perform work, induce change, or bring about a transformation. It is a fundamental concept in physics and is often described as the ability of a physical system to do mechanical, thermal, electrical, or other forms of work. There are multiple definitions for energy, such as:

1. *(noun)- the impetus behind all motion and all activity.*

2. *the ability to do mechanical, thermal, electrical, or other forms of work.*

3. *in physics, a quantity that denotes the ability to do work and is measured in a unit dimensional equivalent.*

4. ***an intangible modified force often characterized as either positive or negative. Believed in some new age religions to emanate from a person place or thing and which can be reserved or transferred in human interactions, shared mood, or group habit or belief- a feeling.***

5. *Eastern orthodox theology- the external actions and influences resulting from an entities internal nature or so by which it is made manifest, as opposed to that internal native self.*

For the purposes of this book, **the fourth definition for energy** is the one that most closely describes **the physical and spiritual energy of consciousness**. The energy of consciousness is often described as vibrational energy or frequency. In truth, the measurement of vibrational frequencies, or energies, of thoughts, feelings, and emotions would be extremely difficult. In the past, **descriptions of such measurements of consciousness have been largely abstract** representations of indirect calculations.

The Measurement of Consciousness Energy

Some scientists have determined they can measure certain frequencies of human actions, including thoughts, emotions, and feelings. These measurements propose the ability to quantify certain emotions using a vibrational or frequency scale. One such scale is *The Vibrational or Emotional Frequency Scale*. (Based on a modified version of The Hawkins Scale of Emotional Consciousness). Use of this scale allows researchers to ascribe a level of energy and vibrational frequency related to different thoughts, emotions, and feelings. (see Chart 1)

The Spectrum of Vibration Frequencies in Human Consciousness-The Hawkins Scale (Frequency-Hz)
Enlightenment and Pure Consciousness - 1000 +
Love, Peace, and Joy - 700-1000
Willingness, Acceptance, Reason (Believe and Receive) - 500-700
Courage and Neutrality (Beginning Consciousness, Awareness) - 250-500
Fear, Worry (Pridefulness, Sin, Ego) - 150-250
Anger (Negative emotional energy, self-destructive thoughts) - 50-150
Guilt, Shame and Apathy (Self-inflicted pain and self-destructive behavior) - 0-50

(Chart 1- The Spectrum of Vibration Frequencies in Human Consciousness)

1.8-The Energy/Power of the Visualized, the Heard, and the Spoken Word

The Visualized Word

'The7Realms' relies heavily on visualizing words. The Bible teaches us to *"read the Word… and study it day and night"*. (Josh 1:8) Normally, to read any word, it must first be **visualized**. The visualization of that word requires a specific amount of energy.

The initial energy required for visualizing the word occurs in the form of light energy traveling through the lens of the eye to the retina which triggers a neuronal (electrical) stimulus.

The neuronal stimulus perceives the word and transmutes the word to the neurons of the brain. In the brain these neurons produce the energy required for this transmutation.

The physical, neuronal, and electromagnetic structure of the brain houses the energy necessary to connect to the mind. So ultimately, it is the mind that perceives and translates the visualization of the word. In this way, the trilateral words of 'The7realms' connect through the conscious mind and subsequently to spiritual consciousness.

The Heard Word and The Spoken Word

In the same way **the spoken word** has a unique energy associated with sound wave energy and sound perception in the mind.

The spoken word generates sound energy which is captured by the tympanic membrane in the ear and transmits that sound wave vibration to the cochlear nerve and subsequently to the brain. Additionally, this sound energy transforms into vibrational energy and is unified with the vibrational energy of the Universe.

Once again, this sound energy is then perceived by the mind, and we become conscious of it. As the spoken word is perceived, it then becomes **the heard word**. And it is the heard word that creates the initial imprint of the perceived word. The Bible describes the Word of God as *"living and powerful…"*. (Heb 4:12)

The Most Powerful Word in the Universe

The most powerful word energy in the Universe comes from the words of the Bible, particularly when they are **spoken**.

The inerrant words of the Bible, when spoken in faith and truth, generate one of the most powerful forces of vibrational energy in the Universe.

Proverbs 18:21 reminds us that *"death and life are in the power of the tongue."*

The power of the tongue represents the energy of the spoken word.

Jesus taught us to use the power of words to speak healing and blessings, not hurt or harm. The greatest healings and blessings come when *we (the children of God)* speak the words of healing and blessing over ourselves and others.

The spoken Word of God has extraordinary power, especially **when it is spoken in the essence of faith by one of His children**. This may be the most powerful word energy in the universe.

When these words are coupled within the context and syntax of their biblical meaning and spiritual purpose, they possess the ability to effect consciousness.

The spiritual power of prayer and meditation combines with the energy of the visualized, the spoken, and the heard word. This power and energy have the ability to indelibly affect consciousness.

One of the key foundational principles in 'The7Realms' is that *the **power and energy of focused prayer and scriptural meditation**, on specific words and scriptures of the Bible, produce the most **powerful spiritual energy** that can transcend the mind, body, and soul and **permeate the highest realms of spiritual consciousness.***

1.9-Thoughts, Feelings, and Emotions (TFEs)

The Energy of Thoughts, Feelings, and Emotions

Different thoughts, feelings, and emotions possess different vibrational energies or frequencies.

The energy of these thoughts, feelings, and emotions often exists in the form of words. Just thinking or speaking a word can emit a certain energy. Once the word is perceived, it is transmuted to the conscious.

Depending on the word and what type of energy or frequency it generates, the level of vibrational frequency can tell you what level of consciousness the word exists within.

Thoughts + Feelings + Emotions = Energy or Vibrational Frequency = Consciousness

For example, the word *love* generates a higher vibrational frequency in your consciousness in comparison to the word *hate*, which generates a lower energy frequency.

The word *peace* generates a higher energy frequency than the word *worry*.

And speaking the name of *God* produces one of the highest of energy frequencies whereas, even thinking the name of *Satan,* evokes one of the lowest of energy frequencies.

(Thoughts + Feelings + Emotions) x Words = Word Energy or Word Vibrational Frequency

A single word, used in the right context, can possess a considerable amount of energy.

But identifying the right group of words arranged together, in the correct pattern or algorithm, can generate an even more powerful and synergistic energy.

The Energy of Thoughts, Feelings, and Emotions as Words

When certain power-filled words are arranged into the correct pattern and placed within the proper energy corridors, they can illuminate bidirectional energy pathways.

Word Energy X Specific Word Patterns (Trilateral) ←→ Spiritual Energy Pathway

These energy paths travel through higher and lower levels of energy frequencies. These energy frequencies represent different levels of consciousness.

More explicitly, when these special words originate from the Bible, they form one of the most powerful energy corridors of all- the corridor, or pathway, to higher consciousness.

Biblical words, when placed together in the correct pattern or arrangement, generate very distinctive energies.

These energies seemed to be based on the contextual power these different words represent or evoke into being.

When biblical words such as *love, peace,* and *joy,* are positioned together, they evoke a different energy frequency than word patterns such as *fear, doubt,* and *worry.*

As I evolved in my study of biblical words in their theological and literal interpretations, I discovered an intriguing pattern between words which evoked similar frequencies.

Through the gift of pattern recognition, I was able to identify seven realms of biblical words and scriptures that equated to distinct levels of spiritual consciousness.

1.10-Prayer and Meditation Evoke Higher Spiritual Energy

The Definition of Prayer

The Oxford dictionary defines **prayer** as:

1) *a solemn request for help or expression of thanks addressed to God or an object of worship;*

2) *a religious service especially a regular one at which people gather to pray together;*

3) *an earnest hope or wish.*

The primary focus of prayer should be to worship, thank, acknowledge, praise, and focus on God. **Prayer equals spiritual energy in action.**

Meditate on 'The Word'

The definition of the word **meditate** is *to think deeply or focus one's mind for a period, in silence or with the aid of chanting, for religious or spiritual purposes or as a method of relaxation.* The definition of meditation is the act of meditating. Synonyms for meditation include *ponder, reflect, deliberate, contemplate, cogitate, and ruminate*.

Focused Prayer + Scriptural Meditation ←→ Prayer-Meditation

Biblical Word Energy (Trilateral Patterns) ←→ 'The7Realms' Spiritual Pathway

A simple explanation for the difference between prayer and meditation, might be to suggest that prayer is us communicating with God, and meditation is listening to God communicate to us.

Prayer-Meditation

For the constructs of this course in 'The7Realms', I have elected to bring together both the words prayer and meditation into a single term- *prayer-meditation*.

Prayer-meditation is the act of combining both the exercise of prayer surrounding specific words and scriptures of the Bible (Christian Mindfulness) along with the practice of meditation on these specific words and scriptures (Biblical Meditation).

This type of meditation facilitates a transcendental excursion from lower realms of spiritual consciousness to higher realms of spiritual consciousness.

'The7Realms' Prayer-Meditation ←→ Christian Mindfulness + Biblical Meditation

Focused prayer and meditation represent energy in the form of **focused spiritual energy**.

Using the trilateral words and scriptures from 'The7Realms' as a guidebook for the practice of prayer-meditation, you can move from one realm, or level of spiritual wellness or consciousness, to another realm or level.

Higher Consciousness = Spiritual Wellness

⬆

Prayer-Meditation

(conscious positive thoughts)

⬆

Lower Consciousness = Spiritual Unwellness

The correct application of positive spiritual energy allows you to emerge from negative subconscious thinking (lower consciousness) and transition to greater spiritual enlightenment (higher consciousness).

These newly defined realms of spiritual consciousness are based on the experience that when we purposefully direct our spiritual energy, in the form of intention (focused prayer or mindfulness) and attention (scriptural meditation), we can ascend to higher consciousness.

In doing so we achieve the transcendental reality of our spiritual being-ness (spiritual consciousness), and we conspire with God to bring our true Self closer to the I AM.

Questions for Week 1/Lesson 1

Week 1: Day 1

What is the **Divine Right of Spiritual Wellness**? What is your understanding of Consciousness? What is your understanding of **Spiritual Consciousness**? How does Spiritual Consciousness relate to **Spiritual Wellness** in 'The7Realms'?

_____
_____
_____
_____
_____
_____
_____
_____
_____
_____
_____
_____
_____
_____
_____
_____
_____
_____
_____

Week 1: Day 2

In *The Ryan Neal story* (my story) how might my childhood experiences with patterns, math, and puzzles have led to my discovery of **trilateral words in the Bible**?

_____
_____
_____
_____
_____
_____
_____
_____
_____
_____
_____
_____
_____
_____
_____
_____
_____
_____

Week 1: Day 3

What is your understanding of Mindfulness? What is the definition of Meditation? What is your understanding of **Christian Mindfulness**? What is your interpretation of **Biblical Meditation**?

_____
_____
_____
_____
_____
_____
_____
_____
_____
_____
_____
_____
_____
_____
_____
_____
_____
_____

Week 1: Day 4

What is the definition of *energy* used in 'The7Realms"? What is **Spiritual Energy?** How might you use Spiritual Energy in meditation to travel to Higher Consciousness?

_____
_____
_____
_____
_____
_____
_____
_____
_____
_____
_____
_____
_____
_____
_____
_____

Week 1: Day 5

What are the different types of **word energy**? [Hint: Is it the *visualized word, the heard word,* or *the spoken word*?] What is considered the **most powerful** 'word energy'? Who is the person who makes it the most powerful 'word energy'?

Week 1: Day 6

How do you think **Thoughts, Feelings, and Emotions (TFEs)** in 'The7Realms' relates to **Vibrational Energy**?

___

Week 1: Day 7

How do you think Prayer, Mindfulness, and Meditation relate to **Spiritual Energy** in 'The7Realms'?

Week 2/Lesson 2: Consciousness Levels and Spiritual Realms

Lesson 2: Consciousness Levels and Spiritual Realms

2.1- The 3 Levels of Consciousness

2.2- The Structure and Organization of 'The7Realms'

2.3- Levels of Consciousness and the Bi-directional Flow of Spiritual Consciousness

2.4- The Explanation of Consciousness Travel or Transcending from Lower Consciousness

2.5- Spiritual Entropy and Quantum Mechanics

2.6- Spiritual Energy and Vibrational Frequency of Consciousness

2.7- Examples of Trilateral Words and Scriptures

Questions for Week 2/Lesson 2

2.1- The 3 Levels of Consciousness

Ryan C. Neal, MD

The **Foundational Structure** of **The Seven Realms** is the **Tetrahedron (3-sided Pyramid)**

Each Pyramid has 3 Levels of Consciousness

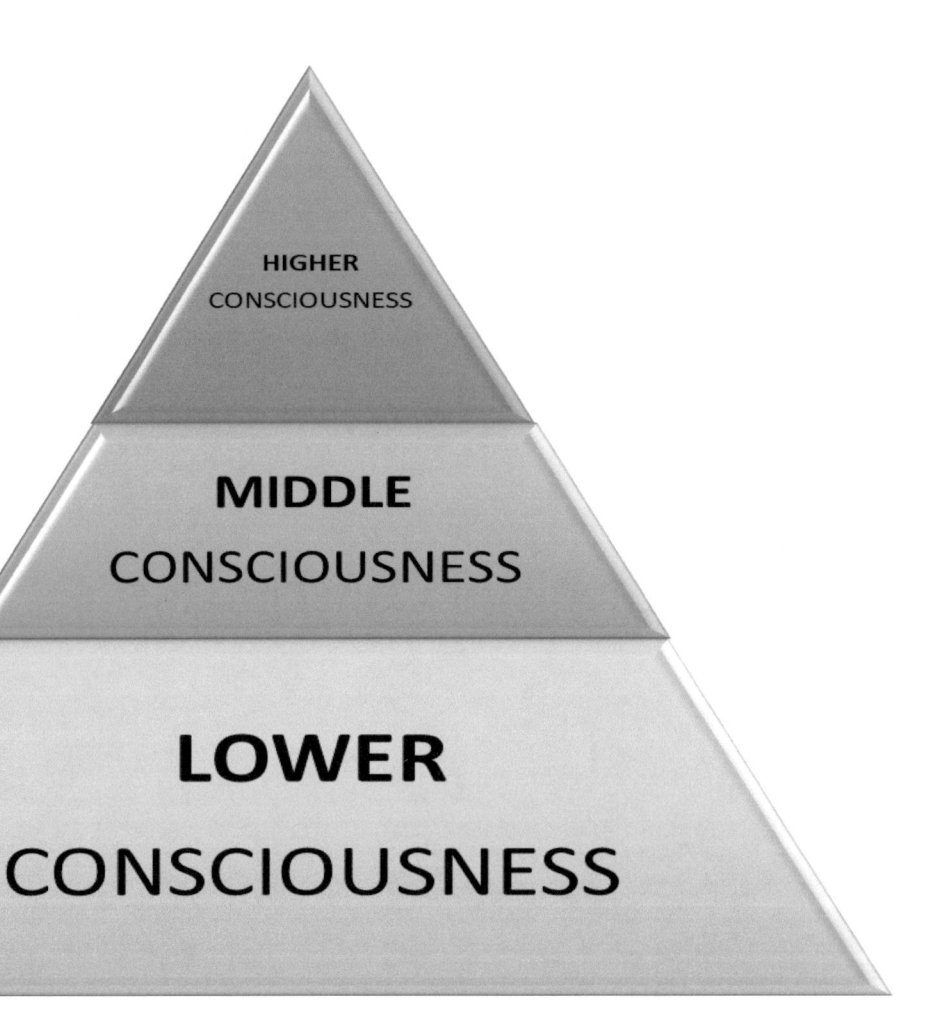

(Diagram 1- The 3 Levels of Consciousness)

The 3 Levels of Consciousness (see Diagram 1)

The first three realms of spiritual consciousness dwell in the level of higher spiritual consciousness.

The biggest problem with expanding our consciousness is that we unfortunately spend the least amount of time, during our waking consciousness, in higher spiritual consciousness. This is largely because higher spiritual consciousness requires the greatest amount of focused energy. If we could redirect even a small amount of our time and energy to our higher spiritual conscious, we could change our entire lives.

The fourth realm of spiritual consciousness represents the middle level of spiritual consciousness, or middle spiritual consciousness.

The middle consciousness level is also known as the middle consciousness realm because it is the only realm in the middle consciousness level.

This fourth realm can act as your initial realm of transition to conscious awakening when we use our spiritual energy to purposefully move out of our lower subconscious thinking.

The last three realms of spiritual consciousness exist in the level of lower spiritual consciousness.

Regrettably we tend to spend far too much time in the largely subconscious realms of lower spiritual consciousness. This generally occurs involuntarily as the lower realms require the least amount of focused spiritual energy and tend to occur naturally because of **spiritual entropy.**

The primary goal of 'The7Realms' is to teach you how to easily redirect your spiritual energy to higher consciousness realms at any given moment.

2.2- The Structure and Organization of The Seven Realms of Spiritual Consciousness- The Pyramid of Sovereignty

The Structure and Organization of
The Seven Realms of Spiritual Consciousness

The Seven Trilateral Realms of **The Pyramid of Sovereignty**:

The First *Trilateral* **Realm of Spiritual Consciousness**

- The Realm of The Trinity- God the Father, God the Son, and God the Holy Spirit

The Second *Trilateral* **Realm of Spiritual Consciousness**

- The Realm of Love, Peace, and Joy- The Realm of "Fruit of The Spirit"

The Third *Trilateral* **Realm of Spiritual Consciousness**

- The Realm of Ask, Seek and Knock-The Realms of Manifestation

The Fourth *Trilateral* **Realm of Spiritual Consciousness**

- The Realm of Mind, Body, and Soul (MBS)- The Mental, The Physical and The Spiritual

The Fifth *Trilateral* **Realm of Spiritual Consciousness**

- The Realm of Self-Condemnation, Fear and Worry

The Sixth *Trilateral* **Realm of Spiritual Consciousness**

- The Realm of Unforgiveness (Hatred), Anger and Doubt

The Seventh *Trilateral* **Realm of Spiritual Consciousness**

- The Realm of Internal Disease, External Disease, and Mental and Psychological Disease- The Realm of Disease Manifestation

(Each Pyramid is made up of 7 Unidimensional Realms- see Illustration 2 on the next page)

Ryan C. Neal, MD

The Structure and Organization of The Seven Realms of Spiritual Consciousness

The Pyramid of Sovereignty
-The Primary Pyramid

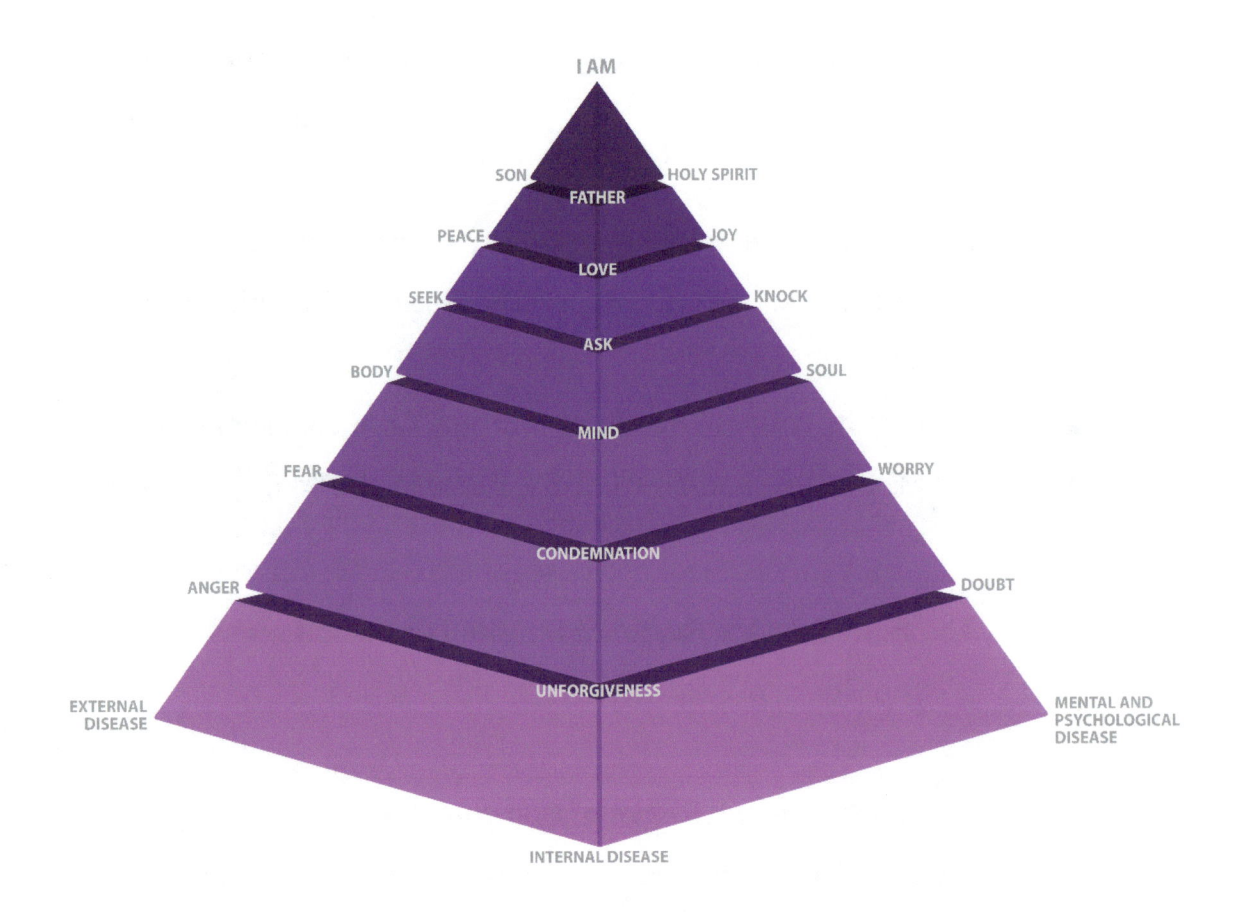

(Illustration 2- The Pyramid of Sovereignty)

The Pyramid of Sovereignty in 'The7Realms'

The Pyramid of Sovereignty represented in The Seven Trilateral Realms of Spiritual Consciousness is the primary pyramid of the four pyramids of 'The7Realms'.

This pyramid is represented as a 3-sided pyramid (a tetrahedron) and is presented as the purple pyramid. In the Bible, *purple symbolizes sovereignty, royalty, sacredness, and prosperity.*

The Sovereignty of God

The Pyramid of Sovereignty refers to the sovereignty of God as the supreme power and authority of God over all things. This belief is foundational to many religious traditions, particularly within Christianity, Judaism, and Islam, with some differences on how God is represented.

As the Supreme Authority, Supreme Being, *God's sovereignty means that He is the highest authority in the universe.*

Everything that happens falls under His governance and will, whether directly caused by Him or allowed to happen within His divine providence.

God's Omnipotence and Omniscience

God's sovereignty is linked to His omnipotence, meaning He is *all-powerful. This is represented in the Pyramid of Sovereignty.*

There is nothing that happens outside of His capability to control or influence. This includes the creation and sustaining of the universe, the course of history, and the details of individual lives. Along with being all-powerful, God's sovereignty implies that He is all-knowing. Meaning He is omniscient. His sovereignty is exercised with full knowledge of the past, present, and future, including every possible outcome of every possible choice.

The Pyramid of Sovereignty and God's Will

The Pyramid of Sovereignty proposes that God causes everything that happens as a part of His divine purpose or will. This includes both His active will (things He causes to happen) and His permissive will (things He allows to happen, even if they result from human free will). Romans 8:28.

For believers, the sovereignty of *God is a source of comfort and assurance* because it means that nothing escapes God's notice or happens outside of His control. It offers a perspective of trust in God's ultimate plan for good, even in the face of suffering and evil.

The Pyramid of Sovereignty and Free Will

Despite God's sovereignty, Christianity also teaches that *we have free will and responsibility*. The relationship between God's sovereignty and human free will is a complex and often deliberated subject.

The prevailing view in many traditions is that while God is sovereign and controls all outcomes, *we (His children) are still allowed to make real choices that have consequences*, and these choices are somehow part of God's sovereign plan.

The Pyramid of Sovereignty and Your Higher Purpose

Mindfulness and meditation practices of 'The7Realms' allows you to consistently approach the sovereignty of God through the trilateral words and scriptures of the Bible. Enabling you to stay in Higher Spiritual Consciousness and access your highest spiritual energy at any given moment.

The mastering of 'The7Realms' occurs from repeated practice of the focused prayers and trilateral scriptural meditations. This mastery of your conscious mind's thoughts, feelings, and emotions, **permits the reprogramming of your subconscious mind to actively default to your higher consciousness.** The ultimate purpose of this practice assists you to live in Gods will for your life. Your higher purpose.

2.3- Levels of Consciousness and the Bi-directional Flow of Spiritual Consciousness

Higher Consciousness Level

The **higher spiritual realms**, or upper realms, in the higher consciousness level, correlate with God consciousness, spiritual virtues, and spiritual manifestation. These realms contain the **1st, 2nd, and 3rd Spiritual Realms.**

These higher realms represent the conscious movement of thoughts, feelings, and emotions through focused prayer and meditation to reach the highest level of spiritual consciousness and subsequently spiritual wellness. In the higher levels are things associated with God consciousness.

The highest state of spiritual consciousness is Oneness with God, full enlightenment, and the awareness of unity with the I AM. (See Diagram 2)

Middle Consciousness Level

The middle consciousness level is equivalent to the **4th Spiritual Realm**, the Realm of Mind, Body, and Soul.

This **middle spiritual realm** is the realm that separates higher consciousness from lower consciousness.

The realm of Mind, Body, and Soul is the spiritual partition that can only be transcended by the practice of focused prayer and meditation.

The middle realm represents the initial awareness of consciousness as *The Self* (self-realization).

Awareness of *The Self* is the consciousness state wherein the spiritual man (spirit) connects with the carnal man (body) in the presence of the soul man (soul).

It is at this intersection that an individual can initiate his or her spiritual energy, through focused prayer and meditation, to ascend to the higher consciousness realms of spiritual wellness. (See Diagram 2)

Lower Consciousness Level

If, however, the appropriate spiritual energy necessary to reach a higher consciousness state is **not** applied, then the passive energy of *spiritual entropy* can take over and pull or coerce you into the lower consciousness states of spiritual *un*wellness. (See Illustration 1-Section 1.6)

The **lower spiritual realms** in the lower consciousness level represent the descension into spiritual unwellness. The **5th, 6th, and 7th Spiritual Realms** reside in the lower level. In the lower levels are things associated with sin consciousness.

The transition occurs through spiritual entropy, the natural descent away from Mind, Body, and Soul, if the appropriate energy is not employed to transcend the coercion of the carnal mind. (See Diagram 2)

Levels of Consciousness and the Bi-directional Flow of Spiritual Consciousness

GOD- THE 'I AM'
GRACE
HEAVEN
LIFE

GOD CONSCIOUSNESS
HIGHER CONSCIOUSNESS
SPIRITUAL WELLNESS
PHYSICAL WELLNESS

THE 1st, 2nd and 3rd REALMS

THE 4th REALM

THE 5th, 6th and 7th REALMS

THE DEVIL
THE LAW
EARTH
DEATH

SIN CONSCIOUSNESS
LOWER CONSCIOUSNESS
SPIRITUAL UNWELLNESS
PHYSICAL DISEASE

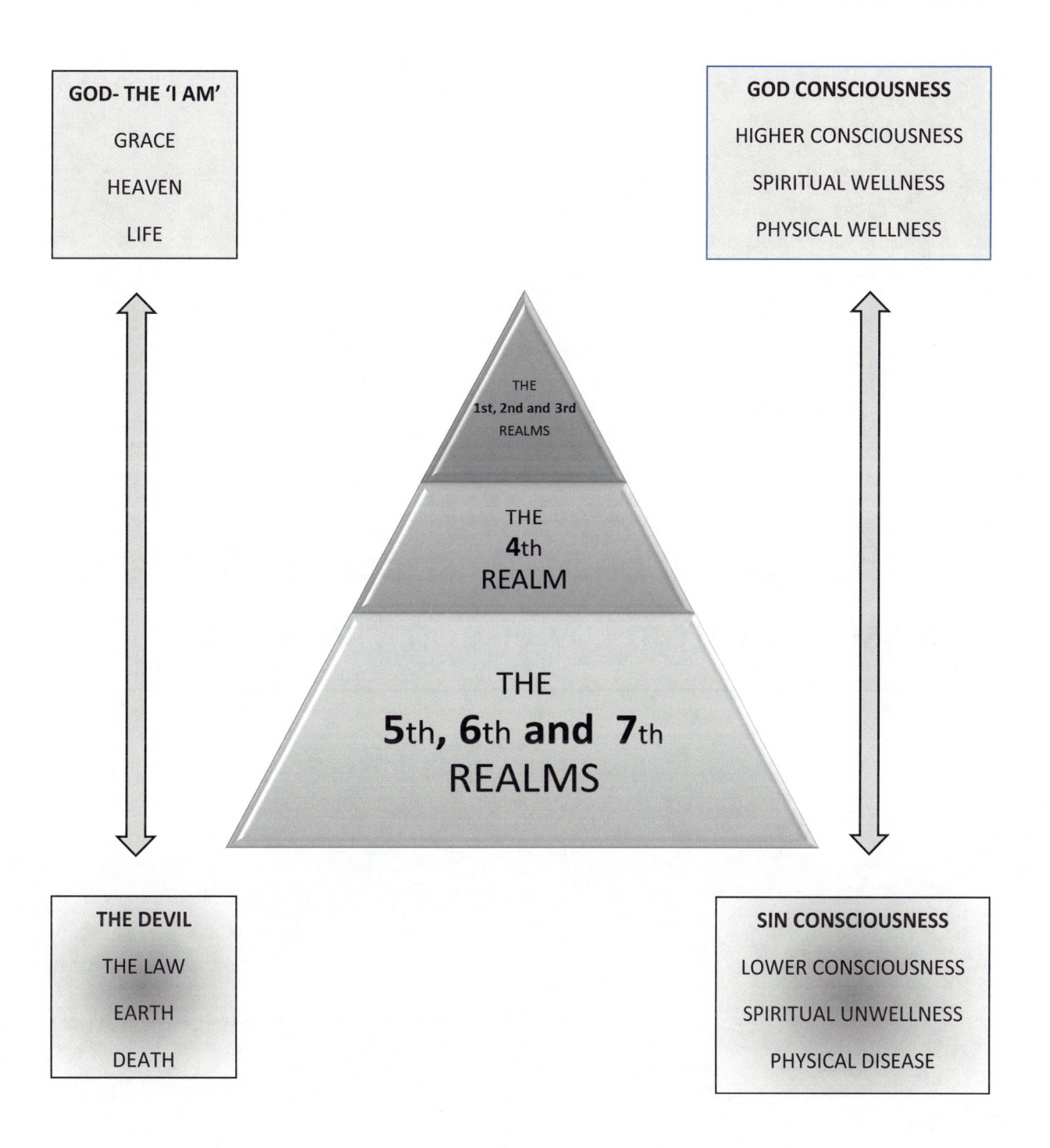

(Diagram 2- The Bi-directional Flow of Spiritual Consciousness)

2.4- The Explanation of Consciousness Travel or Transcending from Lower Consciousness

How Can I Use 'The7Realms' as My Daily Mindfulness and Meditation Practice?

Some people ask, "How do you incorporate 'The7Realms' into your daily practice of mindfulness and meditation?"

The book, **The Seven Trilateral Realms of Spiritual Consciousness**- *A Newly Defined Christian Pathway to Higher Consciousness through Biblical Meditation* (aka 'The7Realms'), is a transformational work that uncovers 84 biblical words and scriptures revealing a hidden pathway to higher consciousness. The ordering and organization of these words and scriptures was given to me as a divine spiritual gift.

This pathway allows us to transcend from our usual states of subconscious thinking (lower spiritual consciousness) to an enhanced state of spiritual enlightenment and spiritual awakening (higher spiritual consciousness) using the newly uncovered **trilateral** words and scriptures from the Bible.

'The7Realms' invites you to travel along this new path to higher spiritual consciousness *(Christian Mindfulness),* by way of focused prayer on these specifically outlined words and scriptures (*Biblical Meditation*).

I chose the word *trilateral* to describe the realms I exposed. The definition of trilateral, as an adjective, means shared by or involving three parties. The word *trilateral* fits with the core basis of my sacred belief in the Trinity.

'The7Realms' acts as a guidebook to direct your mindfulness and meditation practice to transcend to the highest possible spiritual consciousness realm.

Mindfulness and Meditation

I use the phrases *mindfulness and meditation* as terms that outline two separate practices.

Mindfulness is the ability to be aware (*awareness*), or focus, at any given moment, on a specific thought, feeling, emotion, or even a word. In the case of 'The7realms', we use trilateral biblical words or scriptures as centering mantras or prayers.

Mindfulness allows us to center our awareness on these trilateral words or scriptures.

This act of mindfulness doesn't have to be a formal process of pausing and pondering and contemplating on the word. It can simply be the act of becoming mindful of the word or scripture and using that moment of mindfulness to acknowledge the awareness of where this word or scripture resides in your spiritual consciousness.

Mindfulness can be a moment of contemplation to recognize the effect that the word or scripture has on a thought or a feeling or an emotion.

Christian Mindfulness is the act of centering our awareness or focus on the Word of God in the form of *focused prayer (attention).* The trilateral words act as a guidepost or anchoring words, or mantras, to let us know, or remind us, where we exist, at any given moment, in spiritual consciousness, and in which specific realm our thoughts reside.

Meditation on the other hand, is the practice of engaging in a deliberate time and formal process of awareness, or mindfulness, of these divinely ordered trilateral words arranged in a specifically organized progression. The expectation of this meditation practice is the ability to transition through spiritual consciousness to attain higher spiritual consciousness *(intention)*.

The Seven Trilateral Realms of Spiritual Consciousness in descending order are as follows:

- The 1st Realm- The Realm of **The Trinity- God the Father, God the Son, and God the Holy Spirit**

- The 2nd Realm- The Realm of **The Fruit of The Spirit- Love, Peace, and Joy**

- The 3rd Realm- The Realm of **Manifestation- Ask, Seek, and Knock**

- The 4th Realm- The Realm of **Mind, Body, and Soul** *(Middle Consciousness)*

- The 5th Realm- The Realm of **Condemnation, Fear, and Worry**

- The 6th Realm- The Realm of **Unforgiveness (Hate), Anger, and Doubt**

- The 7th Realm- The Realm of **Disease Manifestation- Internal, External, and Mental Diseases**

Each of these realms is made up of a trilateral concept (three inter-related biblical words). Each realm exists within and corresponds to a given level of spiritual consciousness. Each of these biblical words is matched with specific trilateral biblical scriptures.

The use of these trilateral words in this meditation practice instructs us to concentrate our focus on a given realm of spiritual consciousness. This focused intention allows you to rise from a realm of lower consciousness to a realm of higher consciousness.

Based on the discovery of 'The7Realms', this *scriptural meditation (intention)* represents Biblical Meditation. This Biblical Meditation is based on specific trilateral words and scriptures that represent a distinct realm of spiritual consciousness. This practice is meant hopefully to lead to a destination of higher spiritual awareness and enlightenment.

2.5- Spiritual Entropy and Quantum Mechanics

Spiritual Entropy

Remember, spiritual consciousness and spiritual wellness are parallel existences within the realms of conscious thought.

The subconscious and unconscious internal dialogue of lower consciousness thoughts *coerces* you into an entropic state which unknowingly causes you to shift from the state of higher spiritual consciousness to a state of lower spiritual consciousness.

This shift is very subtle. Almost undetectable. This lower state of consciousness evolves into a negative state of spiritual energy and takes on a permissive form of spiritual unwellness.

Unfortunately, this negative downward force of spiritual unwellness tends to occur subconsciously. I call this downward force of subconscious negative energy- *spiritual entropy*.

These lower realms represent a spiritual imbalance, or misdirected energy, which causes movement, or descent, away from the I AM.

Every movement away from the awareness of your true spiritual self- The 'I Am', erodes into your spiritual energy. Subsequently, this descent represents the unintended transition to spiritual entropy and consequently physical disease.

My earlier encounter with the study of quantum mechanics and my new insight into the concept of entropy altered my entire perspective of how spirituality and consciousness might exist in the universe.

The Oxford Dictionary states that entropy is *(1) often interpreted as the **degree of disorder or randomness in the system**; which states that **entropy always increases with time**: and (2) **a lack of order** or predictability; **gradual decline into disorder.***

Thus, disorder would seem to be a potential natural state of the universe, and energy naturally transitions or flows "downward" towards disorder. This natural transition to disorder is called entropy.

Spiritual Entropy and Physical Disease

To maintain order and avoid entropy you must apply a certain amount of opposing energy, in this case positive energy, or higher frequency energy.

Since spiritual entropy follows the same law of quantum physics as natural entropy, higher amounts of positive spiritual energy are required to attain higher spiritual consciousness.

Physical disease is the net effect of spending a protracted period in spiritual entropy.

Disease, both physical and spiritual, is fostered by separation from Source- the I AM.

The farther you journey from the I AM and the longer time you spend in spiritual entropy and the consciousness of *un*wellness, the more likely you are to transition towards physical disease.

The purposeful directing of spiritual energy towards higher spiritual consciousness allows for the transition to spiritual enlightenment and subsequently spiritual wellness.

The evolution to spiritual enlightenment is where the science of medicine and the principles of spirituality join forces in the quantum field to realize the wholeness of healing.

2.6- Spiritual Energy and Vibrational Frequency of Consciousness

Quantum Physics and Vibrational Energy

The energy depicted in quantum physics is often described as vibrational energy.

'The7Realms' correlates with the vibrational energy of human consciousness. (see Chart-2)

The universal paradigm of spiritual consciousness maintains that we are all vibrational energies emerging from the Source. I define that Source as God.

Moreover, this principle says that we have our being-ness in the same existence as the Source of all spiritual energy.

The Energy of Source

We exist within that spiritual energy originating from Source and from that energy we manifest the physical presence of our body.

That physical body is made up of pure energy that can exist in different dimensions or in different realms, including the spiritual realm.

I perceived the words spiritual and consciousness to be supernatural concepts.

These concepts appeared to be represented as realms of consciousness, some unidimensional realms, and some multi-dimensional realms.

Thus, the term *realm* became the best way to define the concept of spiritual consciousness over any other defined spatial construct.

The Energy of Mind, Body, and Soul

The spiritual energy of the universe is connected to the mind, body, and soul through spiritual consciousness.

The spiritual energy of the universe is housed in the I AM. In the I AM is fullness of God and the divine right of spiritual wellness.

The realms of spiritual consciousness are based on the perception that when we direct our spiritual energy, in the form of attention (focused prayer) and intention (scriptural meditation) we ascend to higher consciousness.

In doing so we reach the transcendental reality of our spiritual being-ness (spiritual consciousness), and we conspire with God to bring ourselves closer to the I AM.

And as such, **The Seven Trilateral Realms of Spiritual Consciousness (Spiritual Wellness)** was born.

The Seven Realms of Spiritual Consciousness and The Spectrum of Vibrational Frequencies

(Chart 2 The Vibrational Energy of Spiritual Consciousness and The Seven Realms)

The Seven Trilateral Realms of Spiritual Consciousness (Spiritual Wellness)	The Seven Realms- Highest to Lowest	The Spectrum of Vibration Frequencies in Human Consciousness-The Hawkins Scale (Frequency-Hz)
The Realm of The Trinity - God the Father - God the Son - God the Holy Spirit	The First Realm Highest Realm of Spiritual Consciousness and Spiritual Wellness The Realm of Physical Wellness	Enlightenment and Pure Consciousness - 1000 +
The Realm of the Fruit of The Spirit - Love - Peace - Joy	The Second Realm The Realm of Co-existence in The Spirit	Love, Peace, and Joy - 700-1000
The Realm of Manifestation - Ask - Seek - Knock	The Third Realm The Realm of Physical Manifestation from Spiritual Consciousness	Willingness, Acceptance, Reason (Believe and Receive) - 500-700
The Realm of Consciousness - Mind - Body - Soul	The Fourth Realms The Realm of Spiritual Transition from Lower to Higher Consciousness	Courage and Neutrality (Beginning Consciousness, Awareness) - 250-500
The Realm of Condemnation - Condemnation - Fear - Worry	The Fifth Realm The Initial Realm of Transition into Spiritual Entropy *(The First Realm of Lower Consciousness)*	Fear, Worry (Pridefulness, Sin, Ego) - 150-250
The Realm of Hatred (Self-hatred) - Unforgiveness - Anger - Doubt	The Sixth Realm The Carnal Descent into Lower Consciousness Thoughts, Feeling, and Emotions *(The precursor of physical disease)*	Anger (Negative emotional energy, self-destructive thoughts) - 50-150
The Realm of Disease Manifestation - Internal Disease - External Disease - Mental/Psychological Disease	The Seventh Realm The Lowest Realm of Spiritual Consciousness and Spiritual Unwellness *(The Realm of Physical Disease)*	Guilt, Shame and Apathy (Self-inflicted pain and self-destructive behavior) - 0-50

2.7- Examples of Trilateral Words and Scriptures

The Word of God

The Bible is filled with over 770,000 words making up thousands of passages, verses, or as my grandmother called them, *scriptures.*

As I matured in my own spiritual enlightenment, the Bible revealed itself to me through the appreciation of specific patterns of commonly used biblical words.

Through my gift of pattern recognition, I identified multiple word patterns in the Bible and begin to study their significance.

I concentrated my study around the words which seemed to formulate a pattern of three.

The Scriptures of The Bible

I used the term *scripture* in my everyday practice of prayer and meditation to describe a biblical passage or verse.

I used scripture because it not only implied both the simple meaning of a passage or verse, in the context of its teaching, but also carried the weight of the entire Bible as the Bible can be referred to as the **Scripture** (with a capital 'S').

As I studied the words of the Bible, I saw patterns of three everywhere I looked- from Genesis to Revelation. I also recognized that many of the most notable scriptures were often memorized and/or recited in a cadence of three.

I chose the word *trilateral* to describe these patterns I exposed.

The definition of trilateral, as an adjective, means shared by or involving three parties.

Examples of Trilateral Scriptures:

John 1:1 (NKJV)

1 In the beginning was the Word,/and the Word was with God, / and the Word was God.

Genesis 1: 1-2; 26-27 (NKJV)

The History of Creation

1 In the beginning God created the heavens and the earth./ 2 The earth was without form, and void; and darkness [a]was on the face of the deep./ And the Spirit of God was hovering over the face of the waters.

26 Then God said, "Let Us make man/ in Our image, / according to Our likeness; …

27 So God created man in His own image;/ in the image of God He created him;/ male and female He created them.

Psalm 46:10 (NKJV)

10 Be still, / and know, / that I am God.

Matthew 7: 7 (NKJV)

7 Ask, and it shall be given you;/ seek, and ye shall find;/ knock, and it shall be opened unto you.

Galatians 2:20-21 (NKJV)

20 I have been crucified with Christ;/ it is no longer I who live, / but Christ lives in me;

and the life which I now live in the flesh, / I live by faith in the Son of God, / who loved me and gave Himself for me.

21 I do not set aside the grace of God/ for if righteousness comes through the law,/ then Christ died [a]in vain."

Patterns and Cadences of Three

As I studied these patterns and cadences in the words of the Bible more closely, I developed an increasing curiosity. Were these patterns of three somehow interrelated to the concept of the Trinity?

Did these patterns of three carry the essence of holiness like the Trinity? Were they trying to reveal a yet undisclosed secret hidden amongst the words? I began to look with greater curiosity than ever before.

Biblical words such as *mercy, grace,* and *hope* were occasionally applied in a parallel text to express or convey a message of God's love.

Other words and concepts such as *love, peace, and joy*, were frequently used together and seemed interconnected.

The Trinity

The word trilateral fits with the core basis of my spiritual belief in the Trinity.

The geometric shape for the Trinity is an equilateral triangle where each angle represents the three Godheads of the Trinity and thus, represented a complete *trilateral concept* to me.

The trilateral concept of the Trinity represents divine perfection based on my interpretation of the biblical definition of the number three. Biblically the number three represents divine wholeness and perfection.

Since the Trinity was a comprehensive trilateral concept to me, it became the basic building block for **The Seven Trilateral Realms of Spiritual Consciousness** (aka 'The7Realms').

Example of a Trilateral Scripture and how it Interfaces with 'The7Realms':

Here is an example of what a trilateral scripture looks like and sounds like and why it is considered a three-part scripture. Here is how it interconnects different trilateral words and Realms of Consciousness.

Philippians 4:6 (NKJV)- *"Be anxious for nothing, / but in everything through prayer and supplication, with thanksgiving, / let your requests be made known to God."*

First part

*"Be **anxious** for nothing..."*

[The 5th Realm- The Realm of Condemnation, Fear, and Worry]

Second part

*"but in everything through **prayer and supplication**,*

[The 3rd Realm- The Realm of Ask, Seek, and Knock]

*with **thanksgiving**..."*

[The 2nd Realm- The Fruit of The Spirit]

Third part

*"let your requests be made known to **God**"*

[The 1st Realm- The Realm of The Trinity].

In this trilateral scripture, used as a scriptural prayer-meditation, the practitioner can travel from **The Fifth Realm** of Lower Spiritual Consciousness (LSC) to **The First Realm** of Higher Spiritual Consciousness (HSC).

This trilateral scripture starts with *"Be anxious for nothing..."* - represents **The Fifth Realm**- The Realm of Condemnation, Fear, and Worry.

Then transitions to *"but in everything through prayer and supplication, with thanksgiving."* - **The Third Realm**- representing The Realm of Ask, Seek, and Knock and **The Second Realm**- The Realm of The Fruit of The Spirit.

Finally, the scripture transcends to *"let your requests be made known to God"* – which represents **The First Realm**- The Realm of the Trinity and God-consciousness.

This trilateral scripture is a simple example of the three-part cadence scriptures that I discovered throughout the Bible. These scriptures also contain many of the trilateral words. The Bible is filled with multiple trilateral scriptures and many of them follow the pattern that intertwines trilateral words within these trilateral scriptures.

Example of a Trilateral Scripture and how it Interfaces with 'The7Realms':

For many of these scriptures you can follow the context of the trilateral words through the different realms of spiritual consciousness.

Another example is the continuation of Philippians in verse 4:7 (NKJV)- *"And the peace of God / which surpasses all understanding, / shall guard your hearts and minds through Christ Jesus."*

First part

*"And the **peace** of **God**..."*

[The 2nd Realm- The Realm The Fruit of The Spirit]

[The 1st Realm- The Realm of The Trinity]

Second part

*"which surpasses all **understanding**,"*

[The 4th Realm- The Realm of Mind, Body, and Soul]

Third part

*"shall guard your **hearts and minds**..."*

[The 4th Realm- The Realm of Mind, Body, and Soul]

*"through **Christ Jesus**."*

[The 1st Realm- The Realm of The Trinity]

This example in this trilateral scripture reemphasizes staying in higher consciousness by reiterating *"The Peace of God"* which represents **The Second and First Realms**- The Realm The Fruit of The Spirit and The Realm of The Trinity.

The scripture admonishes us to rise above and stay in higher consciousness by the words *"which surpasses all understanding"*- representing **The Fourth Realm**- The Realm of Mind, Body, and Soul.

Once again transcending to the highest realm through the words *"shall guard your hearts and minds through Christ Jesus..."*- which represents **The Fourth Realm**- The Realm of Mind, Body, and Soul <u>and</u> **The First Realm** - The Realm of the Trinity and Christ-consciousness.

'The7Realms' allows the practitioner of mindfulness and meditation to become uniquely aware of their conscious or subconscious existence based on their Thoughts, Feelings, and Emotions (TFEs) at any given point in time. As such, 'The7Realms' allows them to identify those Thoughts, Feelings, and Emotions and subsequently maintain or transcend above them to Higher Spiritual Consciousness.

Questions for Week 2/Lesson 2

Week 2: Day 1

What are the **3 Levels of Consciousness** described in 'The7Realms'? What is special about the middle level of consciousness?

Week 2: Day 2

Can you write the Seven Realms of Spiritual Consciousness from the highest realm to the lowest realm?

_____
_____
_____
_____
_____
_____
_____
_____
_____
_____
_____
_____
_____
_____
_____
_____
_____

Week 2: Day 3

What do think is meant by the **'bidirectional flow'** of Spiritual Consciousness in 'The7Realms'? What things you might find in the higher level of consciousness? What are the things you might find in the lower level of consciousness?

_____
_____
_____
_____
_____
_____
_____
_____
_____
_____
_____
_____
_____
_____
_____
_____
_____
_____

Week 2: Day 4

What is the difference between Mindfulness and Meditation in 'The7Realms'? What is the difference between Christian Mindfulness and Biblical Meditation in 'The7Realms'?

_____
_____
_____
_____
_____
_____
_____
_____
_____
_____
_____
_____
_____
_____
_____
_____
_____
_____

Week 2: Day 5.

What is the definition of **Spiritual Entropy**? How does Spiritual Entropy relate to the concept of **quantum mechanics**?

Week 2: Day 6

Describe how the different realms in 'The7Realms' might relate to the different levels of energy in the David Hawkins **'Vibrational Frequencies of (Emotional) Consciousness'** scale?

Week 2: Day 7

How does the term *trilateral* relate to The Trinity? What are some examples of *trilateral scriptures* in the Bible?

_____
_____
_____
_____
_____
_____
_____
_____
_____
_____
_____
_____
_____
_____
_____
_____

Week 3/Lesson 3: The Seven Realms

Lesson 3: The Seven Realms

3.1- The Seven Realms

3.2- The Pyramid of Sovereignty -The Primary Pyramid

3.3- The Seven Realms of The Pyramid of Sovereignty

3.4- The 7 Discoveries Related to the Energy and Power of Trilateral Words and Scriptures of the Bible in 'The7Realms'

Questions for Week 3/Lesson 3

3.1- The Seven Realms

The Seven Trilateral Realms of Spiritual Consciousness

The Seven Trilateral Realms of Spiritual Consciousness (aka 'The7Realms') offers an easy-to-follow Christian passageway allowing you to travel from the subconscious state of lower spiritual consciousness to an enlightened state of higher spiritual consciousness.

When you recognize you are in a negative subconscious state, such as anxiety or worry, you can learn to easily engage your spiritual energy to transcend to a more positive state, for instance, peace and joy.

This positive transition can take place by simply redirecting your spiritual energy through focused prayer and meditation to a prespecified state of higher spiritual consciousness.

'The7Realms' guides your mindfulness and meditation practice to achieve this positive transcendental process.

These realms were discovered during my 30-year journey to better understand the words of the Bible and the hidden word patterns in the scriptures that were being revealed to me.

I recognized these newly uncovered word patterns formed triangular realms. I labeled these realms trilateral realms.

I organized these realms into seven realms of spiritual consciousness. There were higher realms and lower realms.

The Seven Trilateral Realms of Spiritual Consciousness

The realms of spiritual consciousness are based on the experience that when we purposefully direct our spiritual energy, in the form of attention (focused prayer) and intention (scriptural meditation), we can ascend to higher consciousness.

In doing so we achieve the transcendental reality of our spiritual being-ness (spiritual consciousness), and we conspire with God to bring our true Self closer to the I AM.

To consistently accomplish this attainment of higher consciousness, we need a reliable spiritual pathway.

Until the discovery of **The Seven Trilateral Realms of Spiritual Consciousness**, no postulate, theory, or concept, has been able to put together the order, sequence, and path, of 'predetermined' words in the Bible, arranged in a specific pattern or order, to achieve higher consciousness.

The simple precepts outlined in this work reveals a newly discovered, multi-dimensional, ordering system of 84 *trilateral* words and scriptures from the Bible, hidden in specific patterns. These patterns reveal the seven realms of spiritual consciousness.

This noteworthy revelation uncovers a distinctive spiritual path, outlined in 'The7Realms', and invites you to travel along this new path to higher spiritual consciousness *(Christian Mindfulness),* by way of focused prayer on the specifically outlined trilateral words and scriptures of the Bible (*Biblical Meditation*).

3.2- The Pyramid of Sovereignty -The Primary Pyramid

Ryan C. Neal, MD

The Structure and Organization of
The Seven Realms of Spiritual Consciousness

The Pyramid of Sovereignty -The Primary Pyramid

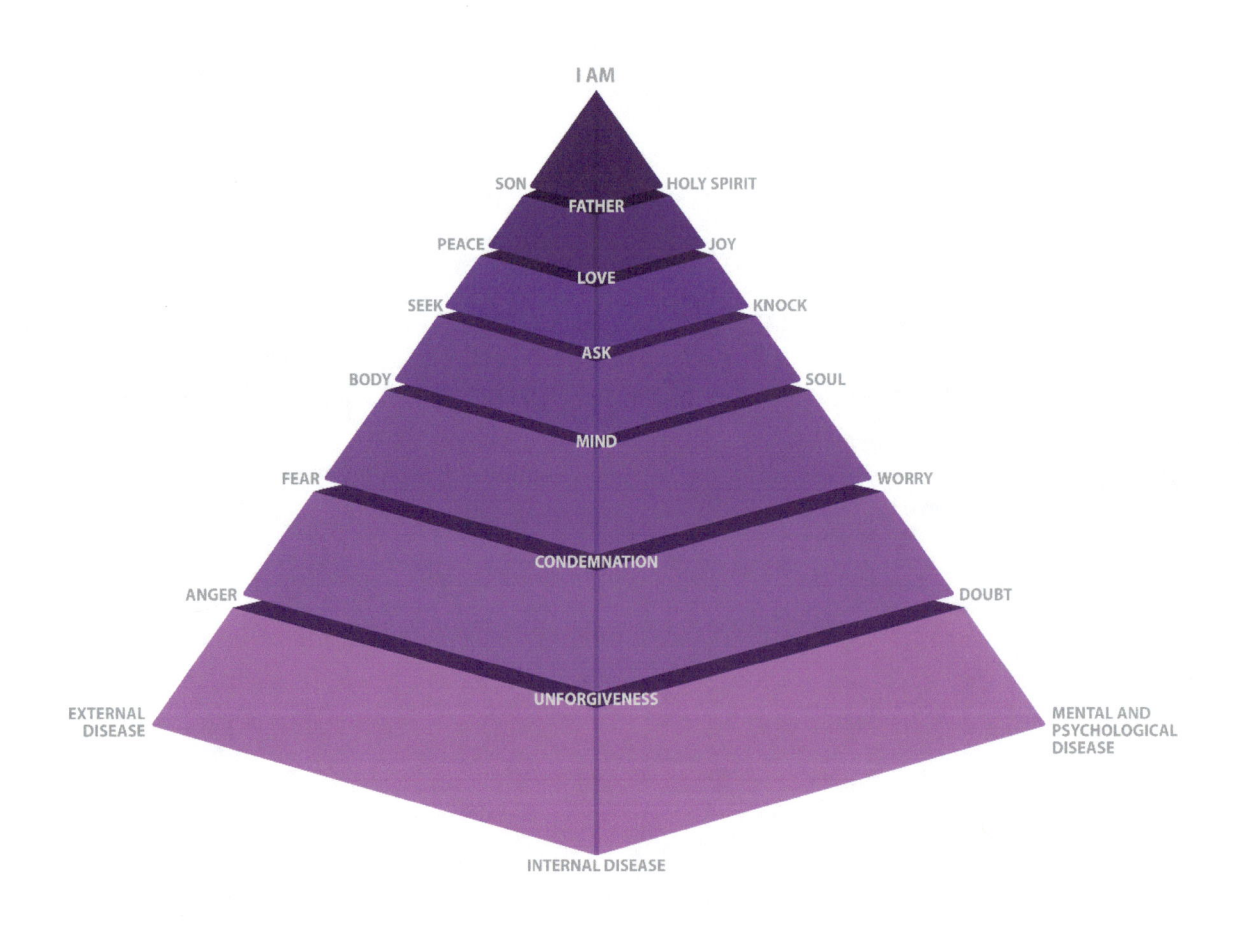

(Illustration 1- The Pyramid of Sovereignty)

3.3- The Seven Realms of The Pyramid of Sovereignty

The Structure and Organization of The Seven Realms of Spiritual Consciousness

The Seven Trilateral Realms of **The Pyramid of Sovereignty:**

The First *Trilateral* **Realm of Spiritual Consciousness**

- The Realm of The Trinity- God the Father, God the Son, and God the Holy Spirit

The Second *Trilateral* **Realm of Spiritual Consciousness**

- The Realm of Love, Peace, and Joy- The Realm of "Fruit of The Spirit"

The Third *Trilateral* **Realm of Spiritual Consciousness**

- The Realm of Ask, Seek and Knock-The Realms of Manifestation

The Fourth *Trilateral* **Realm of Spiritual Consciousness**

- The Realm of Mind, Body, and Soul (MBS)- The Mental, The Physical and The Spiritual

The Fifth *Trilateral* **Realm of Spiritual Consciousness**

- The Realm of Self-Condemnation, Fear and Worry

The Sixth *Trilateral* **Realm of Spiritual Consciousness**

- The Realm of Unforgiveness (Hatred), Anger and Doubt

The Seventh *Trilateral* **Realm of Spiritual Consciousness**

- The Realm of Internal Disease, External Disease, and Mental and Psychological Disease- The Realm of Disease Manifestation

(Each pyramid is made of seven unidimensional pyramids see pages 114 to 128)

The First *Trilateral* Realm of Spiritual Consciousness

The First Trilateral Realms of Spiritual Consciousness

The Realm of the Trinity-
God the Father, God the Son, and God the Holy Spirit

```
        GOD THE FATHER

              △

GOD THE SON        GOD THE HOLY SPIRIT
```

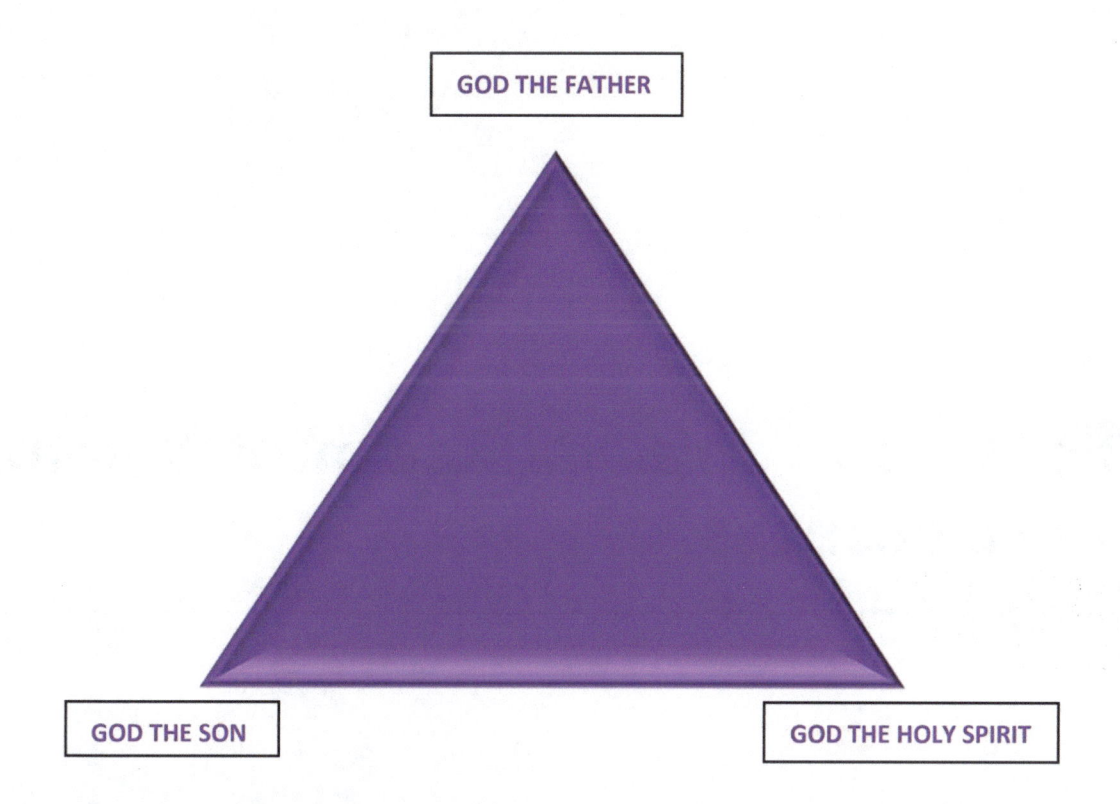

The **First** *Trilateral* Realm of Spiritual Consciousness is the **Realm of the Trinity- God the Father, God the Son, and God the Holy Spirit.** The Realm of The Trinity is the highest of the seven spiritual realms and represents divine unity, spiritual enlightenment, and universal consciousness. Reaching this realm is a prerequisite to attain oneness with The I AM and experience the fullness of God in us.

The Second *Trilateral* Realm of Spiritual Consciousness

The Second Trilateral Realms of Spiritual Consciousness

The Realm of The Fruit of The Spirit- Love, Peace, and Joy

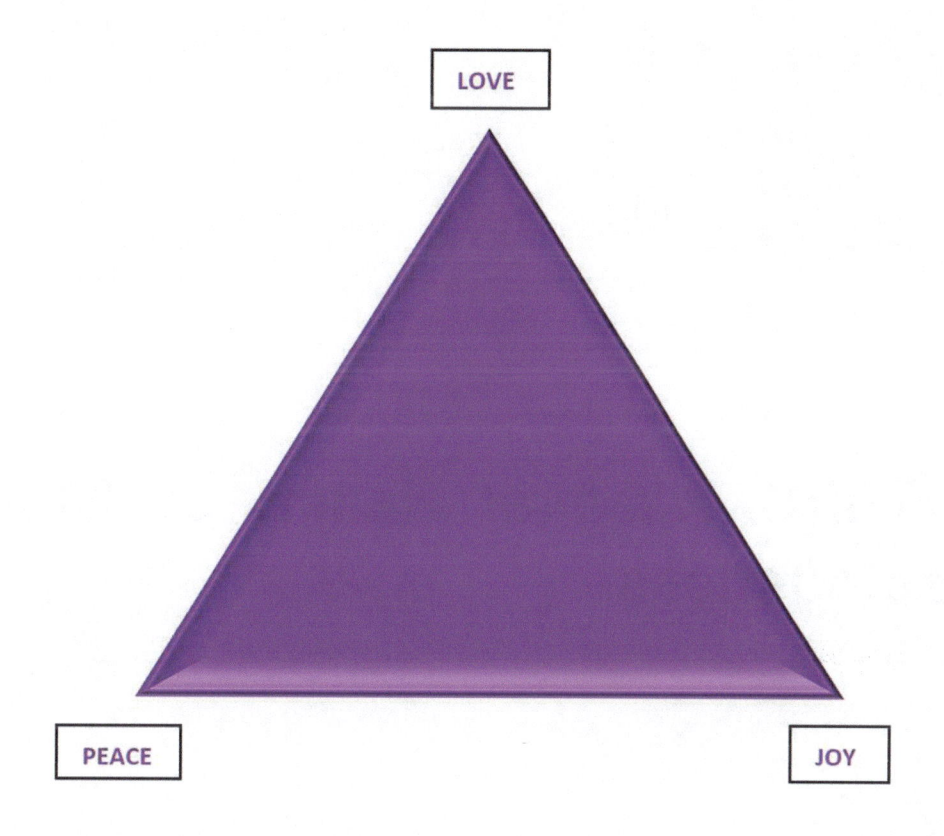

[LOVE]

[PEACE]   [JOY]

The **Second** *Trilateral* Realm of Spiritual Consciousness is the **Realm of Love, Peace, and Joy (LPJ).**
This is the realm where you become aware of the *essence* of the **Fruit of The Spirit**. The second realm of higher spiritual consciousness represents the conscious awareness and spiritual awakening to living in the Spirit.

The Third *Trilateral* Realm of Spiritual Consciousness

The Third Trilateral Realms of Spiritual Consciousness

The Realm of Spiritual Manifestation- Ask, Seek and Knock

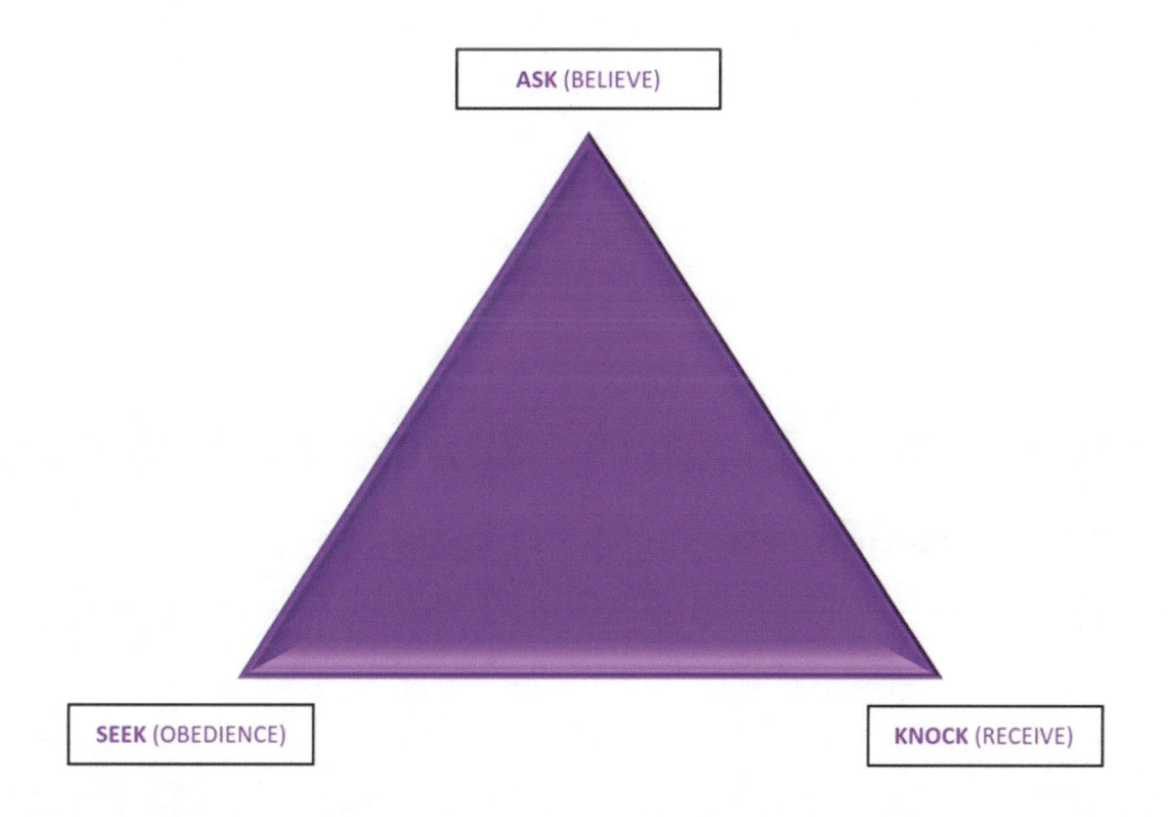

```
            ASK (BELIEVE)

                 /\
                /  \
               /    \
              /      \
             /        \
            /          \
           /            \
          /_____\
  SEEK (OBEDIENCE)    KNOCK (RECEIVE)
```

The **Third** *Trilateral* Realm of Spiritual Consciousness is the **Realm of Ask, Seek and Knock (ASK).** This realm represents the conscious realization of spiritual manifestation. This realm is most exemplified by the biblical scripture,
"Ask and you shall receive, Seek and you shall find, Knock and the door will be open unto you." {Matt 7:7}.

The Fourth *Trilateral* Realm of Spiritual Consciousness

The Fourth Trilateral Realms of Spiritual Consciousness

The Realm of Consciousness- Mind, Body, and Soul

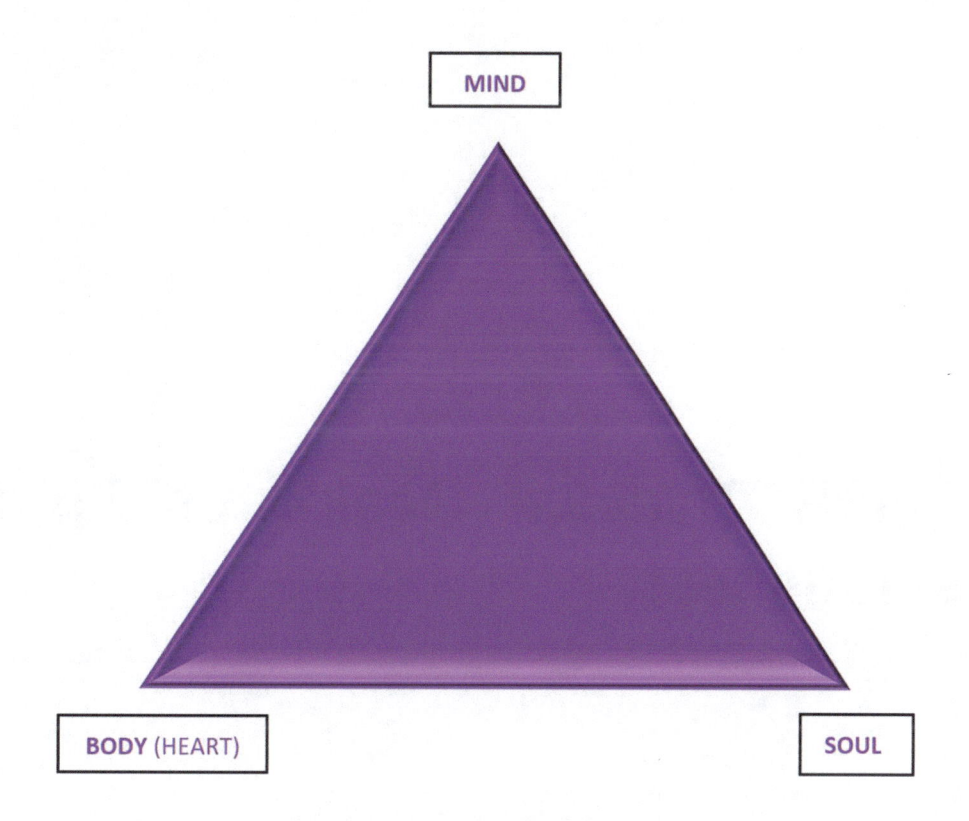

[Triangle diagram with MIND at top, BODY (HEART) at bottom left, and SOUL at bottom right]

The **Fourth** *Trilateral* Realm of Spiritual Consciousness is the **Realm of Mind, Body, and Soul (MBS).** This is the middle realm of spiritual consciousness and acts as the dividing line that *separates* higher consciousness and pure consciousness *from* the subconscious and the unconscious, or the lower consciousness.

The Fifth *Trilateral* **Realm of Spiritual Consciousness**

The Fifth Trilateral Realms of Spiritual Consciousness

The Realm of Condemnation (Lack of Self-Love), Fear, and Doubt

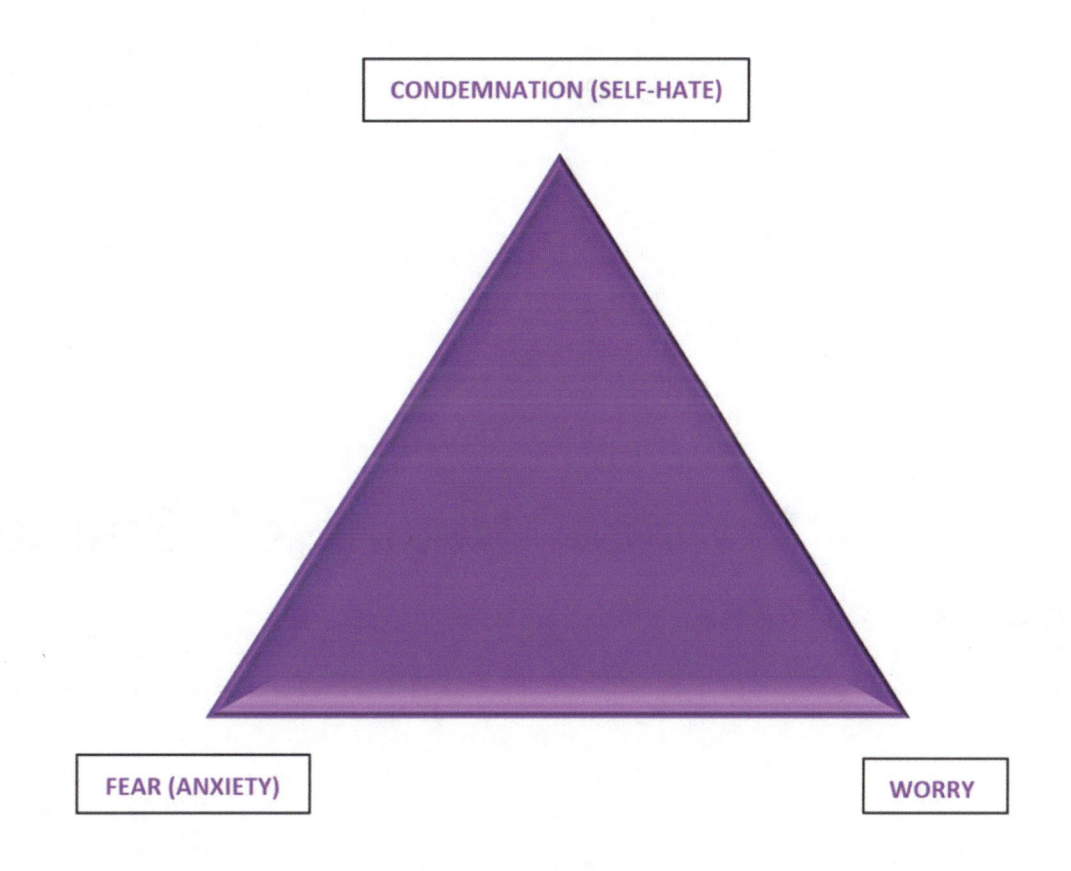

[Diagram: Purple triangle with "CONDEMNATION (SELF-HATE)" at top vertex, "FEAR (ANXIETY)" at bottom-left vertex, and "WORRY" at bottom-right vertex.]

The **Fifth** *Trilateral* Realm of Spiritual Consciousness is the **Realm of Condemnation (Lack of Self-Love), Fear, and Worry (CFW).** This realm is the initial descent into the negative subconscious energy of spiritual unwellness- *spiritual entropy*. In this realm, The Self begins its negative transition from a state of spiritual well-beingness to one of spiritual *un*wellness.

The Sixth *Trilateral* Realm of Spiritual Consciousness

The Sixth Trilateral Realms of Spiritual Consciousness

The Realm of Unforgiveness (Hatred), Anger, and Worry

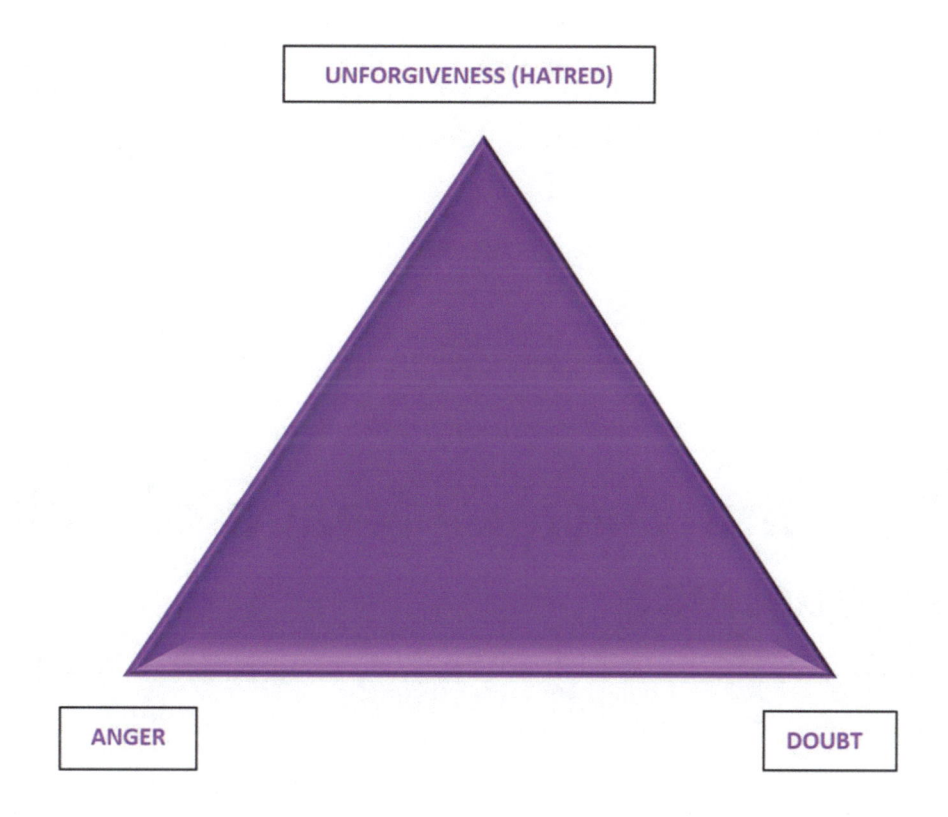

```
         UNFORGIVENESS (HATRED)
                 /\
                /  \
               /    \
              /      \
             /        \
            /          \
           /            \
          /              \
         /_____\
    ANGER                  DOUBT
```

The **Sixth** *Trilateral* Realm of Spiritual Consciousness is the **Realm of Unforgiveness (Hatred), Anger, and Doubt (UAD).** In this realm there is the invasion of the subconscious unrest that progresses from dwelling too long in the *Fifth Realm of Condemnation, Fear and Doubt*. This evolution of *un*wellness is the beginning of the physical manifestation of disease or *dis-ease*.

The Seventh Trilateral Realm of Spiritual Consciousness

The Seventh Trilateral Realms of Spiritual Consciousness

The Realm of Internal, External, and Mental and Psychological Diseases

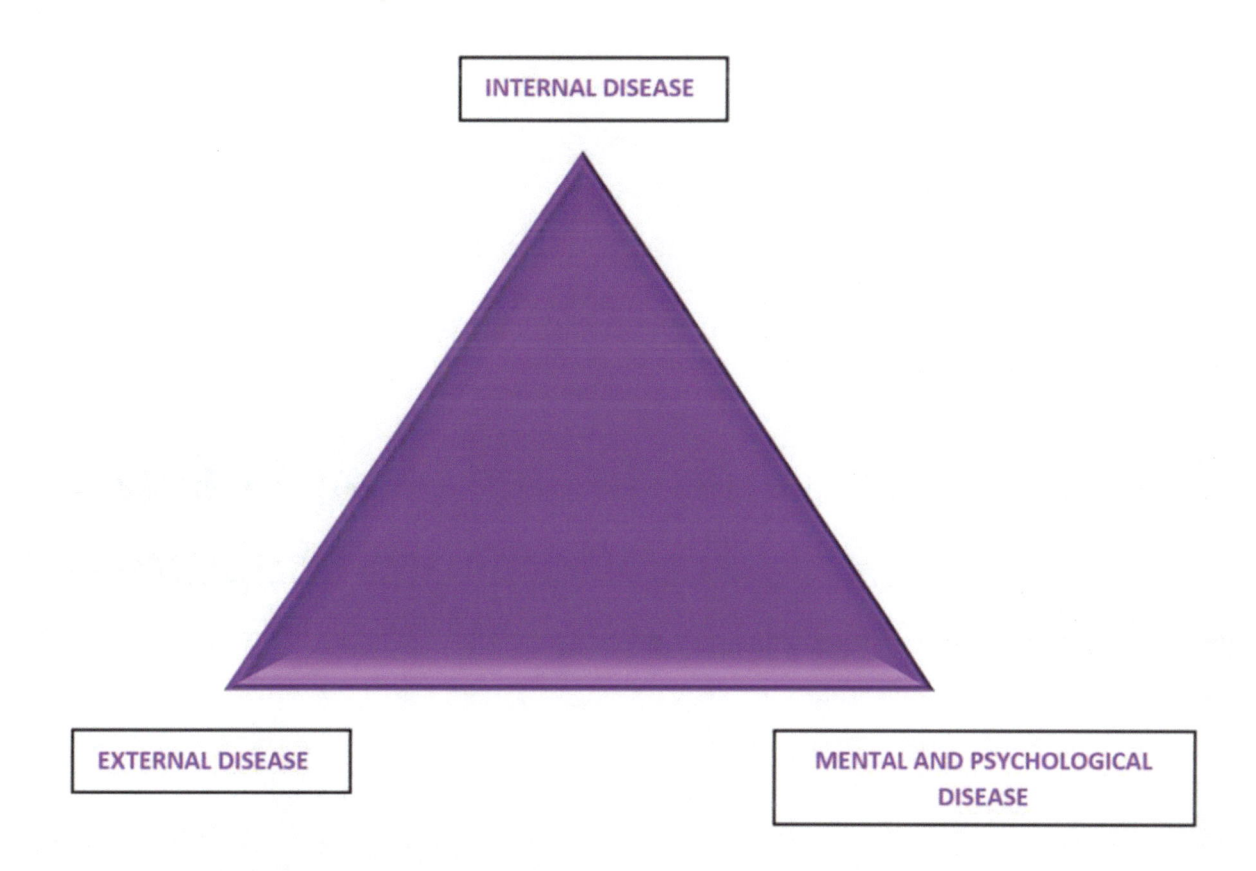

```
              INTERNAL DISEASE

                   /\
                  /  \
                 /    \
                /      \
               /        \
              /          \
             /            \
            /_____\

EXTERNAL DISEASE          MENTAL AND PSYCHOLOGICAL
                                  DISEASE
```

The **Seventh** *Trilateral* Realm of Consciousness is the **Realm of Internal Diseases, External Diseases, and Mental and Psychological Diseases (IEP).** This is the realm of *un*wellness where the culmination of the negative spiritual energy (The Fifth Realm) combines with the negative spiritual and physical energy (The Sixth Realm) to *establish* the manifestation of spiritual and physical *un*wellness that creates physical disease.

3.4- The 7 Discoveries Related to the Energy and Power of Trilateral Words and Scriptures of the Bible in 'The7Realms'

The 7 Discoveries Related to the Biblical Words and Scriptures in 'The7Realms'

Number 1

Specific words and scriptures of the Bible occur in certain patterns that have a **divine alignment**. These words also have an **energy and power** associated with their existence, whether they are read, heard, or spoken. This energy exists within each word and emanates from each word.

Number 2

Specific words in the Bible when put together in a certain pattern (a *trilateral* pattern) have **a unique affiliation with consciousness**. When these words are assembled in this specific pattern, they have **a defined spiritual energy**.

Number 3

When these distinctive words are aligned in a specific pattern, for example, *a trilateral concept or precept*, they have a defined **spiritual energy** and form **a distinctive spiritual realm.**

Number 4

The simplest spiritual realm is a unidimensional realm made up of three separate biblical words or scriptures which align themselves with a similar context/meaning. **When correctly aligned these words or scriptures coalesce to formulate a defined realm within the construct of a distinctive level of spiritual consciousness.** These realms can exist as Higher Consciousness, Middle Consciousness, or Lower Consciousness Realms.

Number 5

Each realm is symbolized by a specific **equilateral triangle and is considered unidimensional**. This triangle represents a separate unidimensional realm within 'The7Realms'.

Number 6

Each unidimensional realm, or trilateral concept, as a separate triangle, exists within one of the **4 Pyramids**. Each Pyramid is geometrically **a tetrahedron (a 3-sided pyramid)** formed by the triangular unidimensional realms. [The name tetrahedron means the sides of the Pyramid are made up of three equilateral triangles and its base is the fourth equilateral triangle.]

Number 7

Each Pyramid has **7 Unidimensional Realms**. There are 4 Pyramids- The Pyramids of **Sovereignty, Restoration, Salvation** and **Truth**. When each Unidimensional Realm of each of the 4 Pyramids coalesces, they create the comprehensive **Multidimensional 7 Realms.**

Questions for Week 3/Lesson 3

Week 3: Day 1

Name **The First Realm of Spiritual Consciousness**. What is your understanding of the meaning and purpose of this realm? Why is this considered the highest realm? How would you describe what **The Trinity** represents?

_____
_____
_____
_____
_____
_____
_____
_____
_____
_____
_____
_____
_____
_____
_____
_____
_____
_____

Week 3: Day 2

Name **The Second Realm of Spiritual Consciousness**. What is your understanding of the meaning and purpose of this realm? What to you think the concept of **The Fruit of The Spirit** represents?

Week 3: Day 3

Name **The Third Realm of Spiritual Consciousness**. What is your understanding of the meaning and purpose of this realm? What do you think it means to '*ask and you shall receive if you believe it in your heart*'?

_____
_____
_____
_____
_____
_____
_____
_____
_____
_____
_____
_____
_____
_____
_____
_____
_____
_____
_____

Week 3: Day 4

Name **The Fourth Realm of Spiritual Consciousness**. What is your understanding of the meaning and purpose of this realm? How do you feel mind, body, and soul related to your spiritual consciousness?

Week 3: Day 5

Name **The Fifth Realm of Spiritual Consciousness**. What is your understanding of the meaning and purpose of this realm? How do you feel condemnation, fear, and worry affect your spiritual consciousness?

_____
_____
_____
_____
_____
_____
_____
_____
_____
_____
_____
_____
_____
_____
_____
_____
_____
_____

Week 3: Day 6

Name **The Sixth Realm of Spiritual Consciousness**. What is your understanding of the meaning and purpose of this realm? How do you think are some examples of how unforgiveness, anger, and doubt can lead to physical disease?

___
___
___
___
___
___
___
___
___
___
___
___
___
___
___
___
___

Week 3: Day 7

Name **The Seventh Realm of Spiritual Consciousness**. What is your understanding of the meaning and purpose of this realm? How might the combination of negative spiritual energy and negative thoughts, feelings, and emotions lead to physical disease?

_____
_____
_____
_____
_____
_____
_____
_____
_____
_____
_____
_____
_____
_____
_____
_____
_____

Week 4/Lesson 4: The First Realm- The Trinity

Lesson 4: The First Realm- The Trinity

4.1- The First Trilateral Realm- The Realm of The Trinity

4.2- The Corresponding Scriptures for The Trinity: God the Father, God the Son, and God the Holy Spirit

4.3- The Definitions of God the Father, God the Son, and God the Holy Spirit

4.4- The Doctrine of The Trinity

4.5- The Spiritual and Biblical Definition of God the Father, God the Son, and God the Holy Spirit

The Exercise- The Mindfulness and Meditation Practice for The First Realm

Questions for Week 4/Lesson 4

4.1- The First Trilateral Realm
The Realm of The Trinity

"A little while longer and the world will see Me no more, but you will see Me. Because I live, you will live also. At that day you will know that I am in My Father, and you in Me, and I in you."

The Structure and Organization of The Seven Realms of Spiritual Consciousness

<u>The Seven Trilateral Realms of **The Pyramid of Sovereignty**:</u>

The First *Trilateral* Realm of Spiritual Consciousness

- The Realm of The Trinity- God the Father, God the Son, and God the Holy Spirit

The Second *Trilateral* Realm of Spiritual Consciousness

- The Realm of Love, Peace, and Joy- The Realm of "Fruit of The Spirit"

The Third *Trilateral* Realm of Spiritual Consciousness

- The Realm of Ask, Seek and Knock-The Realms of Manifestation

The Fourth *Trilateral* Realm of Spiritual Consciousness

- The Realm of Mind, Body, and Soul (MBS)- The Mental, The Physical and The Spiritual

The Fifth *Trilateral* Realm of Spiritual Consciousness

- The Realm of Self-Condemnation, Fear and Worry

The Sixth *Trilateral* Realm of Spiritual Consciousness

- The Realm of Unforgiveness (Hatred), Anger and Doubt

The Seventh *Trilateral* Realm of Spiritual Consciousness

- The Realm of Internal Disease, External Disease, and Mental and Psychological Disease- The Realm of Disease Manifestation

The First Trilateral Realm- *The Realm of The Trinity*

The First *Trilateral* Realm of Spiritual Consciousness is the Realm of the Trinity- God the Father, God the Son, and God the Holy Spirit.

The Realm of The Trinity is the highest of the seven spiritual realms and represents the Realm of God Consciousness.

Reaching this realm is a *prerequisite to attain spiritual enlightenment, Oneness with The I AM and experience the fullness of God in us*.

4.2- The Corresponding Scriptures for The Trinity: God the Father, God the Son, and God the Holy Spirit

The Corresponding Scriptures of God the Father, God the Son, and God the Holy Spirit

Matthew 6: 8-10 (KJV)

*⁸ Be not ye therefore like unto them: for your **Father** knoweth what things ye have need of, before ye ask him. ⁹ After this manner therefore pray ye: **Our Father** which art in heaven, Hallowed be thy name. ¹⁰ Thy kingdom come, Thy will be done in earth, as it is in heaven.*

John 14: 7-11 (KJV)- *The Father Revealed*

⁷ "If you had known Me, you would have known My Father also; and from now on you know Him and have seen Him." ⁸ Philip said to Him, "Lord, show us the Father, and it is sufficient for us."

⁹ Jesus said to him, "Have I been with you so long, and yet you have not known Me, Philip? **He who has seen Me has seen the Father**; so how can you say, 'Show us the Father'? ¹⁰ Do you not believe that **I am in the Father, and the Father in Me?** The words that I speak to you I do not speak on My own authority; but the Father who dwells in Me does the works. ¹¹ Believe Me that **I am in the Father and the Father in Me**, or else believe Me for the sake of the works themselves.

John 14: 15-21 (NKJV)- Jesus Promises Another Helper

¹⁵ "If you love Me, [d]keep My commandments. ¹⁶ And I will pray the Father, and **He will give you another [e]Helper, that He may abide with you forever—** ¹⁷ **the Spirit of truth,** whom the world cannot receive, because it neither sees Him nor knows Him; but you know Him, **for He dwells with you and will be in you.** ¹⁸ I will not leave you orphans; I will come to you.

Indwelling of the Father and the Son

¹⁹ "A little while longer and the world will see Me no more, but you will see Me. Because I live, you will live also. ²⁰ **At that day you will know that I am in My Father, and you in Me, and I in you.** ²¹ He who has My commandments and keeps them, it is he who loves Me. And he who loves Me will be loved by My Father, and I will love him and [f]manifest Myself to him."

4.3- The Definitions of God the Father, God the Son, and God the Holy Spirit

God the Father, God the Son, and God the Holy Spirit

God the Father

God the Father is the first person of the Trinity.

God the Father is the title given to the Sovereign Lord in various religions but specifically in Christianity.

The Father is considered the Creator of all things. God the Father is the source of all things that exist in the universe.

God the Father is the lead *point of enlightenment* in The First Trilateral Realm of Spiritual Consciousness.

God the Son

God the Son is the second person of the Trinity.

God the Son is also given the title of Our Lord and Savior in Christian theology.

Jesus Christ is considered the Son of God in the Trinity and is identified as the incarnation of God. Jesus Christ identifies himself in the essence of consubstantial with God but also distinct and separate as it relates to God the Father and God the Holy Spirit.

God the Son is considered the second point of enlightenment in The First Trilateral Realm of Spiritual Consciousness.

God the Holy Spirit

God the Holy Spirit is the third person of the Trinity.

God the Holy Spirit has been described as the spiritual manifestation of God sent to man as an indoctrination into the Triune with God the father and God the son.

The Holy Spirit has been described as a *helper* sent from the father via the Son to dwell within man. God the Holy Spirit completes the triune of God manifested as God the Father, God the Son, and God the Holy Spirit.

God the Holy Spirit is considered the third *point of enlightenment* in The First Trilateral Realm of Spiritual Consciousness.

4.4- The Doctrine of The Trinity

The 'I Am' and The Trinity

The core ideology of my Christian faith is based on my unwavering belief in the existence of The Trinity. The Trinity constitutes the perfect realm of holiness, or wholeness. In The Trinity we are one with The I Am.

The Trinity represents the spiritual essence that is encompassed in The I Am. While The I Am cannot be fully comprehended or contained, The I Am is the essence of The Trinity.

As spiritual beings we exist within The Trinity and The Trinity exists within us. However, as spiritual beings we are **not** 'The I Am,' but we are *of* the I Am, we are *from* the I Am, and we are *in* the I Am.

The term 'Trinity' does not appear in the Bible and was only introduced to the Christian theology almost two hundred years after the birth of Christ by a theologian named Tertullian. Despite this fact, The Trinity has become the foundational Christian doctrine used to describe the Godhead- God the Father, God the Son, and God the Holy Spirit.

As I matured in my own spiritual enlightenment, the Bible revealed itself to me through the appreciation of specific patterns of commonly used biblical words. I discovered the presence of unique patterns hidden in these recurring words. One of the most common patterns I uncovered in these recurring words was the *pattern of three*.

Subsequently, I observed that many of the most notable biblical scriptures also shared a pattern of three. In the scriptures this pattern appeared as a *cadence of three*. I then recognized that many of these scriptures were often memorized and/or recited in a cadence of three.

I subsequently labeled both the patterns of Biblical words and scriptures with the term **trilateral.** It became increasingly apparent to me that these **trilateral patterns were intimately related to the concept of The Trinity.**

The Doctrine of the Trinity

The doctrine of the Trinity is a fundamental concept in Christian theology that attempts to explain the nature of God as three distinct persons in one divine being. The original explanation of the Trinity has its roots in early Christian thought and the development of theological language over several centuries. It is essential to note that the concept of the Trinity is not explicitly stated in the Bible but is a theological interpretation derived from various biblical passages.

The basic explanation of the Trinity is as follows:

1. **God is One**: The doctrine of monotheism is foundational to Christianity, which means there is only one God. This belief is shared with Judaism and Islam. Christians believe that there is one divine essence, one divine substance or being that is indivisible.

2. **Three Persons**: The doctrine goes on to state that within this one divine being, there are three distinct persons - **Father, Son, and Holy Spirit**. Each person is fully God, co-equal and co-eternal, and yet they are not three separate gods. They are distinct in their roles and relationships but share the same divine nature.

3. **Co-equal and Co-eternal**: The Father, Son (Jesus Christ), and Holy Spirit are equal in their divine nature, attributes, and power. They have existed eternally without beginning or end. None of the three persons is greater or lesser than the other. *Understanding this principle is essential to comprehending our existence as children of God within The Trinity.*

4. **Roles of the Three Persons**:

    - **The Father is the Source** or the begetter of the Son and the Spirit. He is often seen as the Creator and the one who planned salvation.

    - **The Son (Jesus Christ) is the Word of God made flesh**. He took on human form and entered the world to redeem humanity through his sacrificial death and resurrection.

    - **The Holy Spirit is the presence and power of God at work in the world and in the lives of believers**. He convicts, guides, empowers, and sanctifies believers.

The discovery of 'The7Realms' reveals specific trilateral words and scriptures of the Bible that relate to the Trinity. As such, **the Trinity and its three-part essence has become the building block for the mindfulness and meditation practices of 'The7Realms'**. This workbook will take you through understanding the standard definition versus the biblical/spiritual definition of the trilateral words and scriptures identified within the teachings of 'The7Realms'.

4.5- The Spiritual and Biblical Definition of God the Father, God the Son, and God the Holy Spirit

The Spiritual Definitions of God the Father, God the Son, and God the Holy Spirit

The spiritual definitions of God the Father, God the Son (Jesus Christ), and God the Holy Spirit are rooted in Christian theology and the understanding of the Trinity. Keep in mind that interpretations may vary among different Christian denominations.

1. **God the Father:**
    - **Creator**: God the Father is often seen as the Creator of the universe and all that is in it. The belief is grounded in the biblical narrative of God's act of creation as described in the book of Genesis.
    - **Source of Love**: The Father is considered the source of love and the initiator of the divine plan of salvation. In Christian understanding, God's love is so profound that He sent His Son, Jesus, for the redemption of humanity.
    - **Sovereignty**: God the Father is often associated with sovereignty and ultimate authority. He is seen as the one who governs the universe and orchestrates the unfolding of history according to His divine plan.

2. **God the Son (Jesus Christ):**
    - **Incarnation**: The spiritual definition of Jesus Christ involves the concept of the Incarnation, where the eternal Son of God took on human flesh. This is a central theme in Christianity, and it emphasizes God's desire to relate intimately with humanity.
    - **Redemption**: Jesus is seen as the Savior who came to redeem humanity from sin and reconcile people to God. His sacrificial death on the cross is considered the atonement for human sins.
    - **Mediator**: Christ is often understood as the mediator between God and humanity. Through his life, death, and resurrection, Jesus provides a way for people to have a restored relationship with God.

The Spiritual Definitions of God the Father, God the Son, and God the Holy Spirit

3. **God the Holy Spirit:**
   - **Indwelling Presence**: The Holy Spirit is believed to dwell within believers, providing guidance, comfort, and empowerment. This indwelling is seen as a transformative presence, shaping the character and actions of believers.

   - **Conviction and Illumination**: The Holy Spirit convicts individuals of sin, leading them to repentance, and provides illumination for understanding spiritual truths.

   - **Understanding God's Will**: The Spirit is seen as the one who helps believers comprehend God's will and apply it to their lives.

   - **Empowerment for Service**: The Holy Spirit equips believers with spiritual gifts for service in the world. This includes gifts such as prophecy, healing, wisdom, and others, as outlined in the New Testament.

The Trinity is a complex and profound mystery in Christian theology, and these roles of God the Father, God the Son, and God the Holy Spirit are believed to be harmonious and inseparable in their work within the divine unity. The Trinity is the divine and guiding principle linked to the *three-part (trilateral) code* outlining the power of mindfulness and meditation on the newly uncovered trilateral words and scriptures of the Bible.

The Exercise- The Mindfulness and Meditation Practice for The First Realm

Mindfulness and Meditation Practice: Trinitarian Reflection

Combining mindfulness and meditation practices with the spiritual principles of The Trinity—God the Father, God the Son, and God the Holy Spirit—can provide a powerful and enlightening experience. The highest realm of 'The7Realms" is The Trinity. "The7Realms' practice of mindfulness and meditation is as follows: (Spend at least 2-3 mins on each bullet point)

The First Realm- Mindfulness and Meditation- Preparation:

- Setting: Find a quiet and comfortable space. Sit or lie down in a relaxed position.

- Breathing: Begin with a few deep breaths, inhaling slowly through your nose and exhaling through your mouth. Allow your breath to become calm and natural.

The First Realm- Mindfulness and Meditation- God the Father: Creator and Source of Love

- Reflect on Creation: Contemplate the vastness of the universe and acknowledge the Creator, God the Father. Reflect on the beauty and complexity of creation, recognizing it as an expression of divine love.

- Gratitude: Express gratitude for the gift of life and the love that flows from the Creator. Consider specific aspects of your life for which you are thankful.

The First Realm- Mindfulness and Meditation- God the Son: Incarnate Savior and Mediator

- Focus on the Incarnation: Meditate on the idea of God taking on human form in Jesus Christ. Picture the life of Jesus, his teachings, and the sacrifice on the cross. Consider the depth of God's love demonstrated through the Incarnation.

- Personal Reflection: Reflect on your own life and the ways in which the teachings and example of Jesus can be applied to your thoughts, actions, and relationships.

The First Realm- Mindfulness and Meditation- God the Holy Spirit: Indwelling Presence and Empowerment

- Awareness of the Holy Spirit: Shift your attention to the presence of the Holy Spirit within you. Be mindful of the Spirit's role in guiding, comforting, and empowering believers.

- Silent Listening: Spend a few moments in silence, listening to the inner promptings of the Holy Spirit. Allow for a receptive and open heart to discern the Spirit's guidance.

The First Realm- Mindfulness and Meditation- Trinity in Unity: Integration and Gratitude

- Integration: Bring your awareness to the interconnectedness of God the Father, God the Son, and God the Holy Spirit. Recognize the harmony in their work and how they are inseparable in the divine unity.

- Gratitude and Closing: Express gratitude for the time spent in reflection. Close with a prayer or affirmation, acknowledging the Trinity's presence in your life and inviting continued awareness of God's love and guidance.

The First Realm- Mindfulness and Meditation- Closing Thoughts:

This practice integrates mindfulness and meditation with the contemplation of the Trinitarian principles, fostering a deeper connection with the divine. Feel free to adapt the practice to your personal preferences and spiritual journey. Regular engagement with such practices can contribute to a sense of inner peace, spiritual growth, and a greater awareness of the presence of God.

Reminder- As a child of God- *you are of God, you are from God, and you are in God*. You are within The Trinity and The Trinity is within you. You are one with The I Am.

Questions for Week 4/Lesson 4

[Remember to practice **The Mindfulness and Meditation Exercise** associated with this lesson *after completing each daily question*.]

Week 4: Day 1

Define the biblical meaning of **'The Trinity'**. Contemplate the concept of the Trinity. How do you think The Trinity relates to Spiritual Consciousness?

Week 4: Day 2

Contemplate the meaning/concept of **God the Father**. What do you think God Consciousness is?

Week 4: Day 3

Contemplate the meaning/concept of **God the Son**. What do you think Christ Consciousness is?

_____
_____
_____
_____
_____
_____
_____
_____
_____
_____
_____
_____
_____
_____
_____
_____
_____
_____

Week 4: Day 4

Contemplate the meaning/concept of **God the Holy Spirit**. What do you think Spirit Consciousness is? [This is different from Spiritual Consciousness]

_____
_____
_____
_____
_____
_____
_____
_____
_____
_____
_____
_____
_____
_____
_____
_____
_____
_____
_____

Week 4: Day 5

Contemplate the spiritual concept of **'The I Am'**. How might the presence of 'The I Am' relate to the concept of the Trinity and Consciousness in general?

Week 4: Day 6

Contemplate your relationship to **'The Trinity'**. How do you perceive that *you* interrelate or coexist to the essence of The Trinity?

Week 4: Day 7

Contemplate your relationship to **'The I Am'**. How do you perceive your existence within 'The I Am'?

Week 5/Lesson 5: The Second Realm- The Fruit of The Spirit

Lesson 5: The Second Realm- The Fruit of The Spirit

5.1- The Second Trilateral Realms- The Realm of Love, Peace, and Joy

5.2- The Corresponding Scriptures for The Realm of The Fruit of The Spirit: Love, Peace, and Joy

5.3- Understanding The Fruit of The Spirit- Love, Peace, and Joy in 'The7Realms'

5.4- The Standard and the Biblical Definitions of Love, Peace, and Joy

The Exercise- The Mindfulness and Meditation Practice for The Second Realm

Questions for Week 5/Lesson 5

5.1- The Second Trilateral Realm
The Realm of **Love, Peace, and Joy**
"But the fruit of the Spirit is love, peace, joy…; against such there is no law."

The Structure and Organization of The Seven Realms of Spiritual Consciousness

The Seven Trilateral Realms of **The Pyramid of Sovereignty**:

The First *Trilateral* **Realm of Spiritual Consciousness**

- The Realm of The Trinity- God the Father, God the Son, and God the Holy Spirit

The Second *Trilateral* Realm of Spiritual Consciousness

- The Realm of Love, Peace, and Joy- The Realm of "Fruit of The Spirit"

The Third *Trilateral* **Realm of Spiritual Consciousness**

- The Realm of Ask, Seek and Knock-The Realms of Manifestation

The Fourth *Trilateral* **Realm of Spiritual Consciousness**

- The Realm of Mind, Body, and Soul (MBS)- The Mental, The Physical and The Spiritual

The Fifth *Trilateral* **Realm of Spiritual Consciousness**

- The Realm of Self-Condemnation, Fear and Worry

The Sixth *Trilateral* **Realm of Spiritual Consciousness**

- The Realm of Unforgiveness (Hatred), Anger and Doubt

The Seventh *Trilateral* **Realm of Spiritual Consciousness**

- The Realm of Internal Disease, External Disease, and Mental and Psychological Disease- The Realm of Disease Manifestation

The Second Trilateral Realm- *The Realm of **The Fruit of The Spirit***

The **Second** *Trilateral* Realm of Spiritual Consciousness is the **Realm of Love, Peace, and Joy (LPJ).**

This is the realm where you become aware of the *essence* of the **Fruit of The Spirit**. Your love. Your peace. Your joy. Your *Spirit Consciousness*.

The second realm of higher spiritual consciousness represents the conscious awareness and spiritual awakening to living in the Spirit.

5.2- The Corresponding Scriptures for The Realm of The Fruit of The Spirit: Love, Peace, and Joy

The Corresponding Scriptures for Biblical Meditation of Love, Peace, and Joy

Matthew 22 (NKJV) The Scribes: Which Is the First Commandment of All?

34 But when the Pharisees heard that He had silenced the Sadducees, they gathered together. 35 Then one of them, a lawyer, asked Him a question, testing Him, and saying, 36 "Teacher, which is the great commandment in the law?"

*37 Jesus said to him, 'You shall **love** the Lord your God with all your heart, with all your soul, and with all your mind.' 38 This is the first and great commandment.*

*39 And the second is like it: 'You shall **love** your neighbor as yourself.' 40 On these two commandments hang all the Law and the Prophets."*

John 14:26-28 (NKJV)

26 But the [a]Helper, the Holy Spirit, whom the Father will send in My name, He will teach you all things, and bring to your remembrance all things that I said to you.

*27 **Peace** I leave with you, My **peace** I give to you; not as the world gives do I give to you. Let not your heart be troubled, neither let it be afraid.*

28 You have heard Me say to you, 'I am going away and coming back to you.' If you loved Me, you would rejoice because [b]I said, 'I am going to the Father,' for My Father is greater than I.

Psalm 16:11 (NKJV)

*11 You will show me the path of life; In Your presence is fullness of **joy**; At Your right hand are pleasures forevermore.*

5.3- Understanding The Fruit of The Spirit- Love, Peace, and Joy in 'The7Realms'

The Fruit of The Spirit

The Fruit of The Spirit is given to us by God that we may become more like Christ. Through the salvation of Christ, we are given the Fruit of The Spirit that we may emanate the spiritual energy of Christ.

The primary fruits of the spirit are love, peace, and joy.

God is love. Love has no equal thus there is no opposite of love.

Love is mentioned over 300 times in the Bible.

Love is the essence of our existence, our consciousness, and our oneness with God.

Love connects all things. Love conquers all things. Even the word love is powerful.

The word love spoken by a child of God is one of the most powerful and energetic words in the universe.

The thought, feeling, or emotion of love is an energy that emanates from our mind, body, and soul, to the universe and then back to us again.

I believe that if we had the ability to remain in a state of perpetual love, we would never become physical beings but remain in the existence of a spiritual being.

It is my conviction that the one who master's the consciousness of love in this life becomes an eternal spiritual being in the afterlife.

The Fruit of The Spirit

The state or existence of peace is the state or existence that most emulates the presence of Christ on earth.

Christ entered the world to give us peace. The peace of Mind, Body, and Soul

In this peace, we are one with Christ, and Christ is one with us, and we and Christ are one with God.

I believe that the presence of peace in the fruit of the spirit represents our relationship with Christ.

Peace represents the essence of Christ in us.

My peace I leave you, my peace I give you, not as the world gives to you do I give unto you.

Life is a continual search for joy.

The essence of joy that exists in the fruit of the spirit is the true emotion that we chase after but occasionally it is very difficult to attain. Some of us call it happiness, some of us call it bliss, some may call it Nirvana.

I once thought of joy as the same as happiness or the same as euphoria or ecstasy. I now know that joy is much more than just a feeling. Joy is more than simply an emotion or state of being.

Joy is, by definition, the essence of our spiritual journey. Joy is truly the essence of finding oneself within the Holy Spirit.

I believe that in the trilateral concepts in The Seven Trilateral Realms of Spiritual Consciousness- 'Joy' represents the spiritual consciousness of the Holy Spirit in man.

5.4- The Standard and the Biblical Definitions of Love, Peace, and Joy

Standard Definition of Love: The standard definition of love in modern society is typically associated with romantic feelings, attraction, or affection towards someone or something.

It is often characterized by a strong feeling of attachment, desire, or admiration of someone or something. It is often focused on receiving rather than giving and can be conditional and temporary.

Biblical Definition of Love: The biblical definition of love, on the other hand, is much broader and more profound. It encompasses a deep and sacrificial love that is characterized by actions and choices, rather than just emotions or feelings.

Biblical love is based on a selfless and unconditional commitment to the well-being of others, even when it is difficult or costly. This type of love is not based on personal gain, but rather on the desire to serve and bless others.

Love emanates from God as the essence of His relationship to man. God is love.

In 1 Corinthians 13:4-7, the Bible defines love as patient, kind, not jealous, not boastful, not proud, not rude, not self-seeking, not easily angered, and keeping no record of wrongs.

The Bible states that love always protects, always trusts, always hopes, and always perseveres.

This definition emphasizes that love is not just a feeling, but a choice to act in a way that seeks the good of others.

In summary, while the standard definition of love focuses on feelings and personal satisfaction, the biblical definition of love is characterized by selflessness and sacrifice for the benefit of others. It is rooted in the core belief that God is love.

Standard Definition of Peace: The standard definition of peace refers to a state of harmony, tranquility, and absence of conflict or violence.

It is often associated with the absence of war or strife, both on a personal and societal level.

Peace in this context is primarily seen as an external condition or circumstance, where there is a lack of disturbance or unrest.

Biblical Definition of Peace: The biblical definition of peace goes beyond the absence of conflict or violence. It encompasses a deeper and more profound understanding of peace. In the Bible, peace (shalom in Hebrew) is a comprehensive concept that encompasses wholeness, well-being, and harmony in all aspects of life—spiritual, relational, and emotional.

Biblical peace is not just an external condition, but an internal state of being that is rooted in a relationship with God.

Biblical peace is:

1. Peace with God: It refers to being reconciled to God through faith in Jesus Christ. It is the restoration of a broken relationship with God and experiencing His forgiveness, grace, and love.

2. Inner Peace: It is a sense of tranquility and contentment that comes from knowing and trusting in God. It surpasses understanding and guards our hearts and minds in Christ Jesus, even in the midst of difficult circumstances.

3. Peace with Others: Biblical peace calls for reconciliation and harmony in our relationships with others. It involves seeking forgiveness, extending forgiveness, and pursuing peace-making even when it is challenging.

4. Righteousness and Justice: Biblical peace is closely connected to righteousness and justice. It includes working towards social justice, promoting fairness, and advocating for the well-being of others.

In summary, the standard definition of peace focuses on the absence of conflict, while the biblical definition of peace encompasses a holistic and internal state of well-being, rooted in relationship with God, extending to our relationships with others, and reflecting righteousness and justice in the world.

Standard Definition of Joy: The standard definition of joy typically refers to a feeling of happiness, delight, or pleasure.

It is often associated with experiencing positive emotions and a sense of satisfaction or fulfillment.

Joy in this context is primarily seen as a temporary emotional state that is dependent on favorable circumstances or external factors.

Biblical Definition of Joy: The biblical definition of joy goes beyond temporary feelings of happiness. It is a deep and abiding sense of gladness that is not dependent on external circumstances. Biblical joy is rooted in a relationship with God and is considered a spiritual fruit produced by the Holy Spirit within believers.

Biblical joy is:

1. Rooted in God: Biblical joy is based on a relationship with God and is sourced in His presence. It comes from knowing and experiencing God's love, grace, and salvation.

2. Unaffected by Circumstances: Unlike happiness, which is often linked to favorable circumstances, biblical joy is not dependent on external factors. It can be experienced even in the midst of trials, difficulties, or suffering.

3. Foundational in Worship: Biblical joy is expressed in worship and praise to God. It is a response to who God is, His faithfulness, and His work in our lives. It involves rejoicing and exulting in the Lord regardless of our circumstances.

4. Strength and Contentment: Biblical joy provides strength and contentment. It is a source of resilience, enabling believers to endure hardships and challenges. It brings a sense of inner peace and satisfaction that goes beyond momentary happiness.

5. Focused on God's Kingdom: Biblical joy is connected to the anticipation and realization of God's Kingdom. It looks forward to the fulfillment of God's promises and the hope of eternal life with Him.

In summary, the standard definition of joy focuses on temporary feelings of happiness, while the biblical definition of joy is a deep and abiding gladness rooted in a relationship with God. It is not dependent on circumstances and provides strength, contentment, and a focus on God's Kingdom.

Ryan C. Neal, MD

The Exercise- The Mindfulness and Meditation Practice for The Second Realm

A Mindfulness and Meditation Practice for The Second Realm

A mindfulness and meditation practice centered around the mantra of "Love, Peace, and Joy" can be a powerful way to cultivate these positive qualities in your life. Here's a guided meditation practice for you: (Spend at least 5 mins on each section.)

The Second Realm- Mindfulness and Meditation- Setting the Scene:

Find a quiet and comfortable place where you won't be disturbed.

Sit in a comfortable position with your back straight and your hands resting on your lap.

The Second Realm- Mindfulness and Meditation- Centering Yourself:

Begin by taking a few deep breaths in through your nose and out through your mouth. With each breath, let go of any tension or distractions. As you breathe, start to bring your focus inward.

The Second Realm- Mindfulness and Meditation- Introducing the Mantra:

Now, introduce the mantra: "Love... Peace... Joy..." Repeat it softly in your mind. As you say each word, feel its meaning and resonance within you.

The Second Realm- Mindfulness and Meditation- Contemplating Love:

Focus on the word "Love." Visualize a warm, loving energy emanating from your heart. Imagine this love expanding outward, enveloping yourself, your loved ones, and then spreading to include all living beings. With each breath, allow this feeling of love to grow.

The Second Realm- Mindfulness and Meditation- Contemplating Peace:

Shift your focus to the word "Peace." Imagine a sense of calm and tranquillity washing over you like a gentle wave. Feel this peace permeating every cell of your body and spreading into your surroundings. Breathe in peace, breathe out any tension or stress.

A Mindfulness and Meditation Practice for The Second Realm

The Second Realm- Mindfulness and Meditation- Contemplating Joy:

Now, turn your attention to the word "Joy." Visualize a bright, joyful light within you. Feel this light expanding, filling you with a deep and unshakable joy. Let this joy radiate from you to touch the world around you.

The Second Realm- Mindfulness and Meditation- The Integration of Love, Peace, and Joy:

Bring your awareness back to the mantra: "Love... Peace... Joy..." See how these qualities are interconnected. Love leads to peace, and peace nurtures joy. Recognize that you have the power to cultivate and share these qualities in your life.

The Second Realm- Mindfulness and Meditation- Closing Contemplation:

Slowly release the mantra and take a few deep breaths. When you're ready, open your eyes and return to the present moment, carrying the feelings of love, peace, and joy with you.

The Second Realm- Mindfulness and Meditation- Conclusion: Regularly practicing this meditation can help you develop a deeper sense of love, peace, and joy within yourself and extend them to others. Remember that mindfulness and meditation are skills that improve with practice, so be patient and consistent with your efforts.

Questions for Week 5/Lesson 5

[Remember to practice **The Mindfulness and Meditation Exercise** associated with this lesson *after completing each daily question*.]

Week 5: Day 1

Contemplate the biblical concept of '**The Fruit of The Spirit**'.

Week 5: Day 2

Contemplate the concept of the word **Love**. What are some of the differences between the standard definition and biblical/spiritual definition of Love?

___
___
___
___
___
___
___
___
___
___
___
___
___
___
___
___
___
___

Week 5: Day 3

Contemplate the concept of the word **Peace**. What are some of the differences between the standard definition and the biblical/spiritual definition of Peace?

Week 5: Day 4

Contemplate the concept of the word **Joy.** What are some of the differences between the standard definition and the biblical/spiritual definition of Joy?

Week 5: Day 5

Contemplate the **Realm of Love, Peace, and Joy**. How might the Thoughts, Feelings, and Emotions, of Love, Peace, and Joy, have a **synergistic effect** on your Spiritual Consciousness?

Week 5: Day 6

What would it mean to you to be able to **live a greater percentage of your conscious life** in the Higher Spiritual Consciousness **Realm of Love, Peace, and Joy**?

_____
_____
_____
_____
_____
_____
_____
_____
_____
_____
_____
_____
_____
_____
_____
_____
_____

Week 5: Day 7

How do you think **your spiritual well-being would be improved** spending more time in the Spiritual Consciousness of Love? Of Peace? Of Joy? How do you think **your physical well-being would be improved**?

Week 6/Lesson 6: The Third Realm-Manifestation

Lesson 6: The Third Realm- Manifestation

6.1- The Third Trilateral Realm-The Realm of Ask, Seek, and Knock

6.2- The Corresponding Scriptures for The Realm of Manifestation: Ask, Seek, and Knock

6.3- Understanding Manifestation: Ask, Seek, and Knock in 'The7Realms'

6.4- The Standard and the Biblical Definitions of Ask, Seek, and Knock

The Exercise- The Mindfulness and Meditation Practice for The Third Realm

Questions for Week 6/Lesson 6

6.1- The Third Trilateral Realm
The Realm of **Ask, Seek, and Knock**

*"And ye shall seek me, and find me,
when ye shall search for me with all your heart."*

Ryan C. Neal, MD

The Structure and Organization of The Seven Realms of Spiritual Consciousness

The Seven Trilateral Realms of **The Pyramid of Sovereignty:**

The First *Trilateral* **Realm of Spiritual Consciousness**

- The Realm of The Trinity- God the Father, God the Son, and God the Holy Spirit

The Second *Trilateral* **Realm of Spiritual Consciousness**

- The Realm of Love, Peace, and Joy- The Realm of "Fruit of The Spirit"

The Third *Trilateral* Realm of Spiritual Consciousness

- The Realm of Ask, Seek and Knock-The Realms of Manifestation

The Fourth *Trilateral* **Realm of Spiritual Consciousness**

- The Realm of Mind, Body, and Soul (MBS)- The Mental, The Physical and The Spiritual

The Fifth *Trilateral* **Realm of Spiritual Consciousness**

- The Realm of Self-Condemnation, Fear and Worry

The Sixth *Trilateral* **Realm of Spiritual Consciousness**

- The Realm of Unforgiveness (Hatred), Anger and Doubt

The Seventh *Trilateral* **Realm of Spiritual Consciousness**

- The Realm of Internal Disease, External Disease, and Mental and Psychological Disease- The Realm of Disease Manifestation

The Third Trilateral Realm- *The Realm of Ask, Seek, and Knock*

The **Third** *Trilateral* Realm of Spiritual Consciousness is the **Realm of Ask, Seek and Knock (ASK).**

This is the realm of Conscious Manifestation, Faithful Journey, and Spiritual Actualization. *The concept of* ***Asking as if you have already received it.***

This spiritual realm is most exemplified by the *trilateral* biblical scripture, *"Ask and you shall receive, Seek and you shall find, Knock and the door will be open unto you." {Matt 7:7}.*

6.2- The Corresponding Scriptures for The Realm of Manifestation: Ask, Seek, and Knock

The Corresponding Scriptures for Biblical Meditation of Ask, Seek, and Knock

Matthew 7:7-8 (KJV)

⁷ Ask, and it shall be given you; seek, and ye shall find; knock, and it shall be opened unto you:

⁸ For everyone that asketh, receiveth; and he that seeketh, findeth; and to him that knocketh, it shall be opened.

Jeremiah 29:11-13 (KJV)

¹¹ For I know the thoughts that I think toward you, saith the LORD, thoughts of peace, and not of evil, to give you an expected end.

¹² Then shall ye call upon me, and ye shall go and pray unto me, and I will hearken unto you.

¹³ And ye shall seek me, and find me, when ye shall search for me with all your heart.

Mark 11:24 (NIV)

"Therefore, I tell you, *whatever you ask for in prayer, believe that you have received it, and it will be yours.*"

This teaching is also echoed in a slightly different form in the Gospel of Matthew:

Matthew 21:22 (NIV):

"If you believe, you will receive whatever you ask for in prayer."

6.3- Understanding Manifestation: Ask, Seek, and Knock in 'The7Realms'

The Realm of Spiritual Manifestation- Ask

In 'The7Realms' the word **Ask** is the first point of enlightenment in the 3rd Realm. The word **Ask** may be one of the most powerful verbs in the Bible. The word **Ask** appears in the Bible over 200 times.

The Bible is clear that whatever we **Ask** for, in the name of Jesus, it will be given unto us.

"***Ask** anything in my name and it shall be granted unto you.*" **Ask** according to your believing and you shall receive.

"*Whoever **says (ask)** unto this mountain, be thou removed and cast into the sea and believe in his heart without doubting, it shall be done.*"

In the Bible we are told to **Ask** while believing. **Ask** in faith.

The key to manifestation of our spiritual gifts to the world is found in the ***act of Asking.***

In 'The7Realms' the ***act of Asking*** is the secret key to faith. Once you **Ask** you must believe.

"*For he who doubts is like a wave of the sea driven and tossed by the wind that man should not think he would receive anything from God he is a double minded man unstable in all his ways*".

The power of **Ask** is to take the key to faith and put it into the lock of the door of belief and desire. Then opening the door and finding what you dreamt of on the other side.

The Realm of Spiritual Manifestation- Seek

In 'The7Realms' the next step after *Asking* is **Seeking**.

When you *Ask* you must believe that you have already received the thing. And when you believe, you will **Seek** it as if it is already there. You will behave as if you already have it.

Seek is the second point of enlightenment in the 3rd Realm. **Seeking** is the feeling of the manifestation.

Seeking is the belief that you will see *it*, in faith. Believing is the understanding that *it*, already exists.

The Realm of Spiritual Manifestation- Knock

Lastly, in 'The7Realms' you must **Knock. Knock** is the third point of enlightenment in the 3rd Realm.

The act of **Knocking** is taking the *Asking*, or the believing, and the *Seeking*, together as an action of manifestation. **Knocking** is the emotion of the manifestation.

Knocking is the final act of this manifestation as it is the thing already in existence. **Knocking** is the knowing that it is already here.

If you ask for anything and believe that it is already yours, you can close your eyes and visualize that thing, and when you *believe and not doubt*, you will *open your eyes* and it will be there. Once you *Ask*, it is up to you to *Seek* the thing that you *Ask*, **and it will be given unto you**.

6.4- The Standard and the Biblical Definitions of Ask, Seek, and Knock

For the purposes of understanding how 'The7Realms' uses the trilateral words of the Bible, let's compare the standard definitions of "ask," "seek," and "knock" with their biblical meanings.

Standard Definitions:

1. **Ask** (Standard Definition):

    In standard usage, "ask" means to request or inquire about something. It typically involves verbally or in writing expressing a need or seeking information or assistance from someone.

2. **Seek** (Standard Definition):

    To "seek" means to attempt to find, discover, or acquire something. It often involves a conscious effort or action to locate or attain a particular object, goal, or information.

3. **Knock** (Standard Definition):

    "Knocking" refers to the physical action of striking a door or surface with a repeated, rhythmic motion, typically using the knuckles or hands. It is a common way to gain someone's attention or request entry into a closed space.

Biblical Definitions (Matthew 7:7-8):

1. **Ask** (Biblical Definition):

    In the context of Matthew 7:7-8, "ask" takes on a deeper spiritual meaning. It means to bring our needs, desires, and concerns before God in prayer. It signifies recognizing our dependence on God and seeking His intervention in our lives.

2. **Seek** (Biblical Definition):

    Biblically, "seek" extends beyond physical searching. It implies actively pursuing a deeper relationship with God, His presence, and His will. It involves seeking to know God more intimately through study, worship, and a desire for alignment with His ways.

3. **Knock** (Biblical Definition):

    In the biblical context, "knock" represents persistent and determined prayer. It signifies repeatedly and fervently seeking access to God's presence, guidance, and intervention. It's an expression of faith, trust, and the belief that God's door is open to those who earnestly seek Him.

When considering how to use the trilateral words in the mindfulness and meditation practices of 'The7Realms' here are the concepts of "Ask, Seek, and Knock" from a biblical perspective:

1. **Ask** (Matthew 7:7):

   - In the context of prayer, "Ask" means to make requests or petitions before God. It is an invitation to bring our needs, desires, and concerns to Him.

   - Asking in prayer is an acknowledgment of our dependence on God. It reflects humility and a recognition that we cannot navigate life's challenges on our own.

   - This concept emphasizes the importance of open communication with God. We should feel free to approach Him with our requests, both big and small, knowing that He cares for us.

2. **Seek** (Matthew 7:7):

   - "Seek" involves actively pursuing God, His presence, and His will. Seeking God is not merely asking for things but also searching for a deeper understanding of Him.

   - Seeking God implies a desire for intimacy and a longing to know Him better. It means investing time and effort in studying His Word, cultivating a relationship with Him, and striving to align our lives with His principles.

   - This concept emphasizes the idea that a relationship with God is not passive; it requires active engagement and a thirst for spiritual growth.

3. **Knock** (Matthew 7:7):

   - "Knocking" represents persistence in seeking access to God's presence and guidance. Just as knocking on someone's door repeatedly implies determination, knocking in prayer signifies perseverance in seeking God's response.

   - Knocking is an act of faith and trust. It reflects our belief that God's door is open to those who earnestly seek Him, and He is willing to answer our prayers.

   - This concept encourages us not to give up easily in our pursuit of God's will and guidance. It implies that even if our prayers aren't immediately answered, we should continue seeking His presence and direction.

The concept of **"ask as if you have already received"**, is rooted in a biblical teaching found in the New Testament, specifically in the Gospel of Mark and the Gospel of Matthew. It emphasizes a posture of faith and confidence when approaching God in prayer. This may be the most important principle in spiritual manifestation discussed in 'The7Realms'.

The meaning behind the teaching **"ask as if you have already received"** is as follows:

1. **Faith and Confidence**:

    The teaching encourages believers to approach God with faith and confidence in His ability and willingness to answer prayers. It reflects a conviction that God is attentive to our needs and can fulfil our requests.

2. **Believing in Advance**:

    The phrase "believe that you have received it" suggests a forward-looking faith. It's not merely about hoping for a positive outcome but trusting that God has already granted the request even before it becomes apparent in our circumstances.

3. **Aligning with God's Will**:

    The concept encourages aligning our requests with God's will. It assumes that when we pray in accordance with God's purposes and desires, our requests are more likely to be granted. It invites believers to seek God's guidance in their prayers and to desire outcomes that align with His plan.

4. **Persistent Faith**:

    While the teaching emphasizes confidence, it doesn't negate the importance of persistence in prayer. Believers are encouraged to maintain their faith and trust in God even when the answers to their prayers may not be immediately evident.

5. **Relationship with God**:

    This teaching underscores the relational aspect of prayer. It encourages believers to approach God with a sense of intimacy and trust, believing that He cares about their concerns and is actively involved in their lives.

In the teaching of 'The7Realms', "ask as if you have already received" encourages a combination of faith, confidence, and alignment with God's will in prayer. It reflects a relational and faith-filled approach to communicating with God, emphasizing the importance of trust in His ability to answer prayers according to His wisdom and timing.

In The Third Realm- Persistence and a Desire for a Deeper Relationship with God:

- Collectively, "Ask, Seek, and Knock" represent a holistic approach to prayer and spirituality.

- They signify persistence in our pursuit of God. Instead of offering a single prayer and giving up, we are called to continually seek Him and His guidance.

- These actions reflect a deep desire for a relationship with God. We are not content with a superficial connection; we want to know Him intimately and live in alignment with His purposes.

- It also highlights the idea that God is approachable and willing to engage with us. He invites us to ask, seek, and knock, assuring us that He will respond in His wisdom and timing.

In summary, in The Third Realm of Ask, Seek, and Knock from a biblical perspective emphasize the importance of active and persistent engagement with God through prayer and seeking a deeper, more meaningful relationship with Him. These actions demonstrate our dependence on Him, our desire to know Him intimately, and our trust in His willingness to respond to our heartfelt petitions and seek His guidance.

The Exercise- The Mindfulness and Meditation Practice for The Third Realm

A Mindfulness and Meditation Practice for the Third Realm

Mindfulness and meditation can be powerful tools for exploring the concepts of "Ask, Seek, and Knock" in a contemplative and reflective way. Here's an outline for a mindfulness and meditation practice based on these concepts:

Mindfulness and Meditation: Asking, Seeking, and Knocking

Objective: To guide participants in a mindful meditation practice that helps them reflect on the biblical concepts of "Ask, Seek, and Knock," fostering a deeper connection with God and enhancing their prayer life. (Spend at least 2-3 mins on each bullet point)

The Third Realm- Mindfulness and Meditation- Setting and Preparation:

- Find a quiet and comfortable place to sit or lie down.
- Close your eyes gently and take a few deep breaths to relax.

The Third Realm- Mindfulness and Meditation- Centering Yourself:

- Focus your attention on your breath. Feel the rise and fall of your chest or the sensation of your breath entering and leaving your nostrils.
- With each exhale, let go of any tension or distractions.

The Third Realm- Mindfulness and Meditation- Reflecting on the word "Ask":

- In your mind, meditate on the concept of "Ask." Consider the areas of your life where you need guidance, help, or blessings.
- As you inhale, imagine gathering your requests and desires in your heart.
- As you exhale, release these requests to God, acknowledging your dependence on Him.
- Continue this cycle of inhalation and exhalation, focusing on asking God for His presence and intervention in your life.

The Third Realm- Mindfulness and Meditation- Reflecting on the word "Seek":

- Transition your thoughts to the concept of "Seek." Picture yourself on a spiritual journey, seeking God's presence and wisdom.
- Inhale deeply and imagine stepping onto a path toward a deeper connection with God.
- Exhale and visualize yourself drawing nearer to God with each step.
- As you meditate on seeking God, ask Him to reveal Himself to you in new ways.

A Mindfulness and Meditation Practice for the Third Realm

The Third Realm- Mindfulness and Meditation- Reflecting on the word "Knock":

- Shift your attention to "Knock." Envision yourself standing at the door of God's presence.
- Inhale and visualize yourself knocking gently on the door of God's heart.
- Exhale, and with each breath, knock more persistently, signifying your determination to seek His guidance and connection.
- Ask God to open the door to His presence and wisdom as you continue to knock.

The Third Realm- Mindfulness and Meditation- Silence and Listening:

- After reflecting on "Ask, Seek, and Knock," let go of all imagery and simply sit in silence.
- Allow space for God to speak to your heart, whether through thoughts, feelings, or a deep sense of His presence.
- Listen and be open to any insights or guidance that may arise during this time of stillness.

The Third Realm- Mindfulness and Meditation- Closing Contemplation:

- Gently return your awareness to your breath.
- When you're ready, open your eyes and take a moment to reflect on your experience.
- Consider journaling any insights, thoughts, or feelings that arose during the practice.

This mindfulness and meditation practice can help participants connect with the concepts of "Ask, Seek, and Knock" on a deeper level, fostering a sense of spiritual presence and guidance in their lives. It encourages an open and receptive posture toward God's wisdom and direction.

Questions for Week 6/Lesson 6

[Remember to practice **The Mindfulness and Meditation Exercise** associated with this lesson *after completing each daily question*.]

Week 6: Day 1

Contemplate the concept of **'Ask, Seek, and Knock'** (Spiritual Manifestation) as it relates 'The7Realms'.

Week 6: Day 2

Contemplate the meaning/concept of the word **Ask**. What are some of the differences between the standard definition and biblical/spiritual definition of Ask? What is your understanding of the concept ***"ask as if you have already received it"***?

_____
_____
_____
_____
_____
_____
_____
_____
_____
_____
_____
_____
_____
_____
_____
_____
_____

Week 6: Day 3

Contemplate the meaning/concept of the word **Seek**. What are some of the differences between the standard definition and biblical/spiritual definition of Seek?

Week 6: Day 4

Contemplate the meaning/concept of the word **Knock**. What are some of the differences between the standard definition and biblical/spiritual definition of Knock?

Week 6: Day 5

Contemplate the **Realm of Ask, Seek, and Knock**. How might the Thoughts, Feelings, and Emotions, of Ask, Seek, and Knock, have a **synergistic effect** on your Spiritual Consciousness?

Week 6: Day 6

What would it mean to you to be able to live a greater percentage of your conscious life in the **Higher Spiritual Consciousness Realm of Ask, Seek, and Knock**?

_____
_____
_____
_____
_____
_____
_____
_____
_____
_____
_____
_____
_____
_____
_____
_____
_____

Week 6: Day 7

How do you think **your spiritual well-being would be improved** spending more time in the Spiritual Consciousness of Asking? Of Seeking? Of Knocking? How do you think **your physical well-being might be improved**?

Week 7/Lesson 7: The Fourth Realm- The Realm of Middle Consciousness

Lesson 7: The Fourth Realm- The Realm of Middle Consciousness

7.1- The Fourth Trilateral Realm-The Realm of Mind, Body, and Soul

7.2- The Corresponding Scriptures for The Middle Realm of Consciousness: Mind, Body, and Soul

7.3- Understanding the Concept of Mind, Body, and Soul in 'The7Realms'

7.4- The Biblical and Spiritual Concepts of Mind, Body, and Soul

The Exercise- The Mindfulness and Meditation Practice for The Fourth Realm

Questions for Week 7/Lesson 7

7.1- The Fourth Trilateral Realm
The Realm of **Mind, Body, and Soul**

"And you shall love the Lord your God with all your heart, with all your soul, with all your mind, and with all your strength."

Ryan C. Neal, MD

The Structure and Organization of The Seven Realms of Spiritual Consciousness

The Seven Trilateral Realms of **The Pyramid of Sovereignty:**

The First *Trilateral* **Realm of Spiritual Consciousness**

- The Realm of The Trinity- God the Father, God the Son, and God the Holy Spirit

The Second *Trilateral* **Realm of Spiritual Consciousness**

- The Realm of Love, Peace, and Joy- The Realm of "Fruit of The Spirit"

The Third *Trilateral* **Realm of Spiritual Consciousness**

- The Realm of Ask, Seek and Knock-The Realms of Manifestation

The Fourth *Trilateral* Realm of Spiritual Consciousness

- The Realm of Mind, Body, and Soul (MBS)- The Mental, The Physical and The Spiritual

The Fifth *Trilateral* **Realm of Spiritual Consciousness**

- The Realm of Self-Condemnation, Fear and Worry

The Sixth *Trilateral* **Realm of Spiritual Consciousness**

- The Realm of Unforgiveness (Hatred), Anger and Doubt

The Seventh *Trilateral* **Realm of Spiritual Consciousness**

- The Realm of Internal Disease, External Disease, and Mental and Psychological Disease- The Realm of Disease Manifestation

The Fourth Trilateral Realm- *The Realm of Mind, Body, and Soul*

The **Fourth** *Trilateral* Realm of Spiritual Consciousness is the **Realm of Mind, Body, and Soul (MBS).**

The Mind, Body, and Soul Realm exists as a single realm, dedicated as a **transitioning realm,** for the conscious attention (mindfulness) and conscious intention (meditation) on specific *trilateral* words and scriptures.

This realm acts as **a spiritual partition** between the realms that exist as higher consciousness realms and the ones that exist as lower consciousness realms.

7.2- The Corresponding Scriptures for The Middle Realm of Consciousness: Mind, Body, and Soul

The Corresponding Scriptures of Mind, Body, and Soul:

Genesis 2:7 (NKJV) The Garden of Eden

7 And the LORD God formed man of the dust of the ground and breathed into his nostrils the breath of life; **and man became a living being (soul).**

Mark 12:30 (NKJV)

30 And you shall love the Lord your God with all your heart, with all your soul, with all your mind, and with all your strength.' This is the first commandment.

Romans 12:1-2 (KJV)

12 I beseech you therefore, brethren, by the mercies of God, **that ye present your bodies a living sacrifice, holy, acceptable unto God, which is your reasonable service.**

2 And be not conformed to this world: **but be ye transformed by the renewing of your mind**, *that ye may prove what is that good, and acceptable, and perfect, will of God.*

2 Corinthians 4:16 (NKJV) Seeing the Invisible

16 Therefore we do not lose heart. Even though our outward man is perishing, yet the inward man is being renewed day by day.

7.3- Understanding the Concept of Mind, Body, and Soul in 'The7Realms'

The Realm of Mind, Body, and Soul in 'The7Realms'

In 'The7Realms', the middle consciousness level is equivalent to the Fourth Realm, also known as the realm of Mind, Body and Soul.

The Mind, Body, and Soul Realm exists as a single realm, dedicated as a **transitioning realm,** for the conscious attention (mindfulness) and conscious intention (meditation) on specific *trilateral* words and scriptures.

This realm acts as **a spiritual partition** between the realms that exist as higher consciousness realms and the ones that exist as lower consciousness realms.

In other words, this realm serves as a transition zone in 'The7Realms' for mindfulness and meditation when you are travelling from lower consciousness to higher consciousness.

The Realm of Mind, Body, and Soul is the spiritual partition that can only be transcended by the practice of focused prayer and meditations on higher consciousness thoughts, feelings, and emotions.

The middle realm represents the initial awareness of consciousness as *The Self* (self-realization).

In 'The7Realms' awareness of *The Self* is the consciousness state **wherein the spiritual man (spirit) connects with the carnal man (body) in the presence of the soul man (soul).**

It is at this intersection that an individual can use his or her **spiritual energy**, through the focused prayers and meditations of 'The7Realms', to transcend to the higher consciousness levels of spiritual wellness.

If, however, the appropriate spiritual energy to reach a higher consciousness state is **not** applied, then 'The7Realms' describes how the passive energy of *spiritual entropy* takes over and pulls or coerces you into the lower consciousness states of spiritual *un*wellness.

In 'The7Realms' the **lower spiritual realms** in the lower consciousness level represent the transition into spiritual unwellness.

The transition occurs through spiritual entropy, the natural descent away from Mind, Body, and Soul if the appropriate energy is not employed **to transcend the coercion of the carnal mind.**

7.4- The Biblical and Spiritual Concepts of Mind, Body, and Soul

Spiritual and Biblical Concepts of the Mind, Body, and Soul in 'The7Realms'

Spiritual and biblical concepts of the mind, body, and soul are intertwined but may have different nuances depending on the religious or philosophical tradition. Here, we will provide a general comparison, primarily focusing on the Judeo-Christian perspective:

Mind in 'The7Realms':

Spiritual Perspective: In many spiritual traditions, including some Eastern philosophies, the mind is often seen as a complex and integral part of an individual's consciousness. It is associated with thoughts, emotions, and consciousness itself. Spiritual practices often aim to quiet the mind, achieve mental clarity, and attain a state of inner peace or enlightenment.

Biblical Perspective: The Bible doesn't explicitly differentiate between the mind and the soul as modern psychology does. Instead, it often uses the term "heart" to encompass both intellectual and emotional aspects. There are references to renewing the mind (Romans 12:2), having a sound mind (2 Timothy 1:7), and thinking on virtuous things (Philippians 4:8).

Body in 'The7Realms':

Spiritual Perspective: The body is generally seen as the physical vessel or temple that houses the soul or consciousness. Many spiritual traditions emphasize the importance of caring for the body, often through practices like yoga, meditation, and mindful eating, to facilitate spiritual growth and well-being.

Biblical Perspective: In the Bible, the body is regarded as a creation of God and is meant to be treated with respect. The New Testament often emphasizes that the body is a temple of the Holy Spirit (1 Corinthians 6:19-20), and believers are encouraged to present their bodies as a living sacrifice (Romans 12:1).

Spiritual and Biblical Concepts of the Mind, Body, and Soul in 'The7Realms'

Soul in 'The7Realms':

Spiritual Perspective: The concept of the soul varies across spiritual traditions. In many Eastern philosophies and some Western mystical traditions, the soul is seen as eternal and distinct from the physical body and mind. It is often believed to reincarnate through various lifetimes. Achieving a deep understanding of the soul and its connection to the divine is a central goal in these traditions.

Biblical Perspective: In the Judeo-Christian tradition, the soul is often equated with the essential, eternal, and immaterial aspect of a person. It is created by God and is distinct from the body and mind. The soul is believed to be the seat of one's individuality, consciousness, and moral responsibility. Concepts of salvation and the afterlife are closely tied to the fate of the soul.

Conclusion:

The concepts of mind, body, and soul hold profound significance in both biblical and spiritual perspectives.

While there are common themes, such as the importance of mindfulness and the connection between the three elements, there are also distinct interpretations and practices associated with each tradition.

Exploring these concepts can deepen one's understanding of their spiritual journey and their relationship with the divine.

Theology of Wholeness: Mind, Body, and Soul in Biblical Teaching and God Consciousness

The interconnection between the mind, body, and soul is a foundational concept within Christian theology, reflecting the holistic nature of human existence as designed by God.

These three aspects are deeply interwoven in the Bible's teachings, each playing a essential role in the believer's journey toward God consciousness—a state of awareness and alignment with God's will and presence.

This discussion explores how the mind, body, and soul relate to the principal teachings of the Bible and contribute to the cultivation of God consciousness.

Mind: The Spirit of Renewal and Discernment in The Fourth Realm

In biblical teaching, the mind is more than just the center of intellectual activity; it is the seat of transformation and discernment. Paul exhorts believers in Romans 12:2 to "be transformed by the renewing of your mind."

This renewal is not merely about acquiring new knowledge but about fundamentally altering one's thought patterns to align with God's will. The mind, therefore, becomes a battleground for spiritual warfare (Ephesians 6:12), where believers are called to reject worldly influences and embrace divine wisdom.

The mind's role in God consciousness is essential. A renewed mind discerns God's will, understands His purposes, and fosters a deeper relationship with Him. Philippians 4:8 further instructs believers to think about "whatever is true, noble, right, pure, lovely, admirable," emphasizing that a mind focused on these virtues is attuned to God's character.

By cultivating such a mindset, believers can live out the reality of God's kingdom here on earth, symbolizing His love and righteousness in their thoughts and actions.

Body: The Temple of the Holy Spirit in The Fourth Realm

The body, according to biblical teaching, is not merely a physical shell but a sacred vessel of the Holy Spirit. In 1 Corinthians 6:19-20, Paul reminds the Corinthians that their bodies are "temples of the Holy Spirit," urging them to honor God with their bodies. This perspective elevates the body to a place of sacred importance, requiring believers to maintain purity, health, and respect for their physical form.

Theologically, the body's sanctity is tied to the doctrine of the Incarnation, where Jesus Christ took on human flesh, thereby affirming the goodness of the human body. By caring for our bodies, we acknowledge and honor this divine affirmation. Furthermore, the body is integral to the practice of God consciousness.

Through acts of worship, physical service, and the embodiment of Christ-like virtues, believers demonstrate their commitment to God's will. Whether through fasting, prayer, or acts of kindness, the body becomes a conduit for expressing divine love and holiness.

Soul: The Eternal Essence and Center of Worship in The Fourth Realm

The soul, within biblical theology, is the eternal essence of a person, created in the image of God (Genesis 1:27). It is at the core of identity, will, and moral consciousness.

Jesus underscores the soul's value in Matthew 16:26, asking, "What good will it be for someone to gain the whole world, yet forfeit their soul?" This rhetorical question highlights the soul's utmost importance over worldly achievements.

The soul's relationship with God is the core of God consciousness. It is through the soul that believers experience the depth of their connection with God, engage in worship, and seek spiritual growth. Psalm 103:1 encapsulates this beautifully: "Bless the Lord, O my soul; and all that is within me, bless His holy name."

Worship, prayer, and ethical living are expressions of a soul aligned with God's spirit, reflecting a life dedicated to His glory and purposes.

Integration: A Holistic Approach to God Consciousness in The Fourth Realm

The integration of mind, body, and soul is crucial for cultivating a holistic God consciousness. This integration reflects the biblical principle of shalom, a state of comprehensive peace and wholeness.

Each aspect—mind, body, and soul—must be nurtured and aligned with God's will to achieve this state.

1. **Mind:** Engage in regular study of the scripture, prayerful reflection, and mental discipline to align thoughts with God's truth.

2. **Body:** Practice healthy living, self-control, and use the body to serve others and glorify God through acts of compassion and worship.

3. **Soul:** Foster deep spiritual practices, such as worship, prayer, and ethical living, to nurture the soul's connection with God.

In doing so, believers embody the fullness of life that Jesus promised (John 10:10), living in a state of constant awareness and alignment with God's presence and purposes.

This holistic approach not only enriches personal spirituality but also enhances the witness of the Christian community, demonstrating the transformative power of living in agreement with God's design.

Conclusion: The Mind, The Body, and The Soul in The Fourth Realm

The theological discussion of mind, body, and soul within the framework of biblical teachings and God consciousness reveals a profound interconnectedness designed by God. Each aspect plays a vital role in the believer's spiritual journey, and their integration leads to a life that reflects God's glory and grace.

By nurturing and aligning the mind, body, and soul with God's will, believers can achieve a state of holistic well-being and divine awareness, representing the fullness of life that God intended.

Ryan C. Neal, MD

The Exercise- The Mindfulness and Meditation Practice for The Fourth Realm

The Mind-Body-Soul Mindfulness and Meditation Practice of 'The7Realms'

A spiritual mindfulness and meditation practice that focuses on the aspects of mind, body, and soul, drawing inspiration from relevant trilateral biblical words and scriptures:

The Objective of 'The7Realms' Mindfulness and Meditation is to align your mind, body, and soul with the wisdom and guidance of biblical teachings, fostering spiritual growth and inner peace. (Spend at least 2-3 mins on each bullet point.)

Instructions:

The Fourth Realm- Mindfulness and Meditation- Preparation:

- Find a quiet and comfortable space where you can sit or kneel.
- Close your eyes gently and take a few deep, intentional breaths to center yourself.
- Invite the presence of God and the Holy Spirit into your meditation.

The Fourth Realm- Mindfulness and Meditation- Contemplate the Concept of Mind:

- Begin by focusing on your mind.
- Meditate on the following scripture: "Do not conform to the pattern of this world but be transformed by the renewing of your mind. Then you will be able to test and approve what God's will is—his good, pleasing, and perfect will." (Romans 12:2, NIV)
- Reflect on what it means to renew your mind in alignment with God's will. How can you let go of worldly influences and align your thoughts with His wisdom and love?

The Fourth Realm- Mindfulness and Meditation- Contemplate the Concept of Body:

- Shift your focus to your body.
- Meditate on the following scripture: "Or do you not know that your bodies are temples of the Holy Spirit, who is in you, whom you have received from God? You are not your own; you were bought at a price. Therefore, honor God with your bodies." (1 Corinthians 6:19-20, NIV)
- Consider how you can honor God with your body through self-care, health, and mindful living. Reflect on the stewardship of your physical self as a temple of the Holy Spirit.

The Mind-Body-Soul Mindfulness and Meditation Practice of 'The7Realms'

The Fourth Realm- Mindfulness and Meditation- Contemplate the Concept of Soul:

- Turn your attention to your soul.
- Meditate on the following scripture: "Bless the Lord, O my soul, and all that is within me, bless his holy name!" (Psalm 103:1, ESV)
- Allow this verse to inspire gratitude and praise from the depths of your soul. Express your love and devotion to God, acknowledging His presence within you.

'The Fourth Realm- Mindfulness and Meditation- Integration of Mind, Body, and Soul:

- Bring your awareness back to the unity of mind, body, and soul.
- Meditate on the scripture: "Love the Lord your God with all your heart and with all your soul and with all your mind." (Matthew 22:37, NIV)
- Imagine a divine light enveloping your entire being, harmonizing your thoughts, physical sensations, and the essence of your soul.
- Feel a profound sense of love and devotion for God, recognizing His presence in every aspect of your existence.

The Fourth Realm- Mindfulness and Meditation- Closing Thoughts:

- Slowly open your eyes, maintaining a sense of peace and spiritual connection.
- Take a moment to offer a prayer of gratitude and commitment to God.
- Carry this sense of alignment with your mind, body, and soul into your daily life, seeking to live in accordance with His will and grace.

Note: This meditation draws on key biblical passages to encourage reflection, alignment, and devotion to God in all aspects of your being. These biblical passages are interconnected to the trilateral words and scriptures associated with the 4th Realm- The Realm of Mind, Body, and Soul. Regular practice can deepen your spiritual connection and bring about a sense of inner peace and purpose.

Questions for Week 7/Lesson 7

[Remember to practice **The Mindfulness and Meditation Exercise** associated with this lesson *after completing each daily question*.]

Week 7: Day 1

Contemplate the concept of **'Mind, Body, and Soul'**. How does this concept relate to **Middle Spiritual Consciousness** in 'The7Realms'?

Week 7: Day 2

Contemplate the meaning/concept of the word- **Mind**. What are some of the differences between the standard definition and biblical definition of Mind?

Week 7: Day 3

Contemplate the meaning/concept of the word- **Body**. What are some of the differences between the standard definition and biblical definition of Body?

Week 7: Day 4

Contemplate the meaning/concept of the word- **Soul**. What are some of the differences between the standard definition and biblical definition of Soul?

Week 7: Day 5

Contemplate the **Realm of Mind, Body, and Soul**. How might the Thoughts, Feelings, and Emotions, of Mind, Body, and Soul, have a **synergistic effect** on your Spiritual Consciousness?

Week 7: Day 6

What would it mean to you to be able to **live a greater percentage of your conscious life** in the Higher Spiritual Consciousness **Realm of Mind, Body, and Soul?**

___
___
___
___
___
___
___
___
___
___
___
___
___
___
___
___
___
___
___

Week 7: Day 7

How do you think **your spiritual well-being would be improved** spending more time in the Spiritual Consciousness of the transitional realm of Mind, Body, and Soul? How do you think **your physical well-being might be improved**?

_____
_____
_____
_____
_____
_____
_____
_____
_____
_____
_____
_____
_____
_____
_____
_____
_____
_____
_____

Week 8/Lesson 8: The Fifth Realm- Condemnation, Fear, and Worry

Lesson 8: The Fifth Realm- Condemnation, Fear, and Worry

8.1- The Fifth Trilateral Realm- The Realm of Condemnation, Fear, and Worry

8.2- The Corresponding Scriptures for The Realm of Condemnation, Fear, and Worry

8.3- Understanding the Concepts of Condemnation, Fear, and Worry in 'The7Realms'

8.4- Contemplating the Biblical and Spiritual Concepts of Condemnation, Fear, and Worry

The Exercise- The Mindfulness and Meditation Practice for The Fifth Realm

Questions for Week 8/Lesson 8

8.1- The Fifth Trilateral Realm
The Realm of **Condemnation, Fear, and Worry**
"There is therefore now, no condemnation…"

Ryan C. Neal, MD

The Structure and Organization of The Seven Realms of Spiritual Consciousness

The Seven Trilateral Realms of **The Pyramid of Sovereignty:**

The First *Trilateral* **Realm of Spiritual Consciousness**

- The Realm of The Trinity- God the Father, God the Son, and God the Holy Spirit

The Second *Trilateral* **Realm of Spiritual Consciousness**

- The Realm of Love, Peace, and Joy- The Realm of "Fruit of The Spirit"

The Third *Trilateral* **Realm of Spiritual Consciousness**

- The Realm of Ask, Seek and Knock-The Realms of Manifestation

The Fourth *Trilateral* **Realm of Spiritual Consciousness**

- The Realm of Mind, Body, and Soul (MBS)- The Mental, The Physical and The Spiritual

The Fifth *Trilateral* Realm of Spiritual Consciousness

- The Realm of Self-Condemnation, Fear and Worry

The Sixth *Trilateral* **Realm of Spiritual Consciousness**

- The Realm of Unforgiveness (Hatred), Anger and Doubt

The Seventh *Trilateral* **Realm of Spiritual Consciousness**

- The Realm of Internal Disease, External Disease, and Mental and Psychological Disease- The Realm of Disease Manifestation

The Fifth Trilateral Realm- *The Realm of **Condemnation, Fear, and Worry***

The **Fifth** *Trilateral* Realm of Spiritual Consciousness is the **Realm of Condemnation (Self-condemnation), Fear, and Worry (CFW).**

This realm is the *initial descent into the negative subconscious energy* of spiritual unwellness- **spiritual entropy**.

In this *trilateral* realm The Self begins its negative transition from a state of spiritual wellness to a state of **spiritual *un*wellness**.

8.2- The Corresponding Scriptures for The Realm of Condemnation, Fear, and Worry

The Corresponding Scriptures of Condemnation, Fear, and Worry

Romans 8:1 (KJV)

*8 **There is therefore now no condemnation** to them which are in Christ Jesus, who walk not after the flesh, but after the Spirit.*

Psalm 27:1-2 (KJV)

*27 The L*ORD* is my light and my salvation; **whom shall I fear**? the L*ORD* is the strength of my life; of whom shall I be afraid?*

Isaiah 41:10 (NKJV)

*10 **Fear not, for I am with you**: Be not dismayed, for I am your God.*

I will strengthen you, Yes, I will help you, I will uphold you with My righteous right hand.

Matthew 6:25-34 (NKJV) *Do Not Worry*

[25] "Therefore I say to you, **do not worry about your life, what you will eat or what you will drink; nor about your body, what you will put on. Is not life more than food and the body more than clothing?** [26] Look at the birds of the air, for they neither sow nor reap nor gather into barns; yet your heavenly Father feeds them. Are you not of more value than they? [27] Which of you by worrying can add one [a]cubit to his [b]stature?

8.3- Understanding the Concepts of Condemnation, Fear, and Worry in 'The7Realms'

The Realm of Condemnation, Fear, and Worry

The Fifth Realm of Spiritual Consciousness is the first of the *subconscious realms*. As such, this realm often initiates the unintended, negative and downward transition away from the Higher Spiritual Consciousness Realms (the First, Second, and Third Realms).

<u>**Reminder**</u>: In 'The7Realms', the dividing realm between *higher* spiritual consciousness, or spiritual wellness, and *lower* spiritual consciousness, or spiritual unwellness, is the Realm of Consciousness known as **The Fourth Realm- The Realm of Mind, Body, and Soul (MBS).**

The Realm of Consciousness immediately below **The Fourth Realm** is **The Fifth Realm- The Realm of Condemnation, Fear, and Worry (CFW)**. The Fifth, Sixth, and Seventh Realms of 'The7Realms' make up the Lower Spiritual Consciousness Realms.

These realms are considered *subconscious realms*, as they often exist largely in subconscious thoughts. These realms also represent things the Bible instructs us **not** to do. Such as: *"there is no condemnation"; "do not fear"; "do not worry"*.

This downward transition away from Higher Spiritual Consciousness is called **spiritual entropy**. Unaware of this often-subtle subconscious, or even unconscious, transition away from consciousness or higher consciousness, we can easily slip into negative subconscious realms and dwell in these realms too long and return far too often.

The Fifth Realm is the realm of consciousness which *initiates the spiritual descent into spiritual unwellness*.

The Fifth Realm is the first realm where we begin our *carnal descent into spiritual entropy*.

The Fifth Realm is by far the most common point of entry for negative subconscious descent and the most common place for our negative subconscious Thoughts, Feelings, and Emotions (TFEs) to reside.

The Realm of Condemnation, Fear, and Worry

Condemnation

Self-condemnation, or condemnation of others, easily slips into our Thoughts, Feelings, and Emotions (TFEs) daily. As self-condemnation, it may show up in the form of guilt and shame. In condemnation of others, it is often in the form of judgement.

Condemnation is one of the most cunning tools of the devil. He sometimes uses this tool by deceptively attaching it to righteousness. We might inappropriately confuse our self-condemnation with the acknowledgement, or self-punishment for what we deem an unrighteous act.

Forgetting that we have already received forgiveness from God. Or we might self-righteously condemn the act of another, feeling a sense of righteousness thinking to ourselves, *"I would never do such a thing."*

Fear

The most common negative emotion that any of us can experience is fear.

The concept of fear can exist as a person, a place or thing. The word fear can be a verb or a noun. Fear can exist as a thought, a feeling, an emotion or all three.

Fear can enter our lives at any given moment, from any given direction, and at any given time. Fear knows no boundaries.

Fear has its own distinct vibrational energy. That energy is manifestly negative.

Thoughts, feelings, and emotions of fear can come on slowly and subtly or instantaneously. When this occurs instantaneously, fear can come as a sharp, strong emotional burst that pierces our vibrational core like an explosion.

Fear has one of the largest bandwidths of negative vibrational energy and can easily pull the subconscious mind into its expansive vortex. Fear must be dealt with up front and early on to avoid its unintended consequences of self-destructive behavior- emotional and physical. Remaining out of this downward force of negative spiritual energy requires a constant vigilance of attention and intention on positive spiritual energy.

This is accomplished through mindfulness and meditation in 'The7Realms'.

If we are not cognizant of the pervasive nature of fear at all times, it can easily lead us in a downward spiral to the next lower consciousness realm- The Sixth Realm of Spiritual Consciousness- The Realm of Hatred (Unforgiveness), Anger, and Doubt.

The Realm of Condemnation, Fear, and Worry

Worry

Lastly, The Fifth Realm of Spiritual Consciousness constitutes thoughts, feelings, and emotions surrounding the word- worry.

This word in the trilateral realm of The Fifth Realm is almost always a salient combination of the other words, or concepts, condemnation, and fear.

Worry is primarily an internal emotional state characterized by apprehension, uneasiness, or nervousness about future events or outcomes.

Worry is the combination of fear that something at any given moment can or will happen that is bad or negative. Worry can become a chronic condition.

It involves mental and emotional rumination, where individuals repeatedly think about, dwell on, or anticipate negative outcomes or difficulties.

In spirituality, worry is often contrasted with trust in God. It conveys the idea that excessive worry can reflect a lack of trust in God's providence, care, and control over one's life and circumstances.

The spiritual perspective on worry reassures individuals that God knows their needs and cares for them. It encourages trust in God's provision and guidance.

8.4- Contemplating the Biblical and Spiritual Concepts of Condemnation, Fear, and Worry

Standard Definition of Condemnation and Self-Condemnation:

The everyday use of the word **condemnation** is primarily understood as a negative judgment or strong disapproval of someone's actions, behavior, beliefs, or moral choices. It often involves societal or legal judgment and may lead to social exclusion or legal consequences. Some notable definitions or descriptions are as follows:

1. Moral or Ethical Judgment: Condemnation often carries moral or ethical connotations. It is a way to express disapproval of actions or behaviors that are considered socially unacceptable or unethical.

2. Legal Context: Condemnation can also be used in legal settings, where it refers to the formal judgment or declaration of someone being guilty of a crime or wrongdoing, leading to penalties or punishment.

3. Social and Public Expression: Condemnation is often publicly expressed, either through verbal statements, written communication, or social and cultural norms. It can result in social shaming and ostracism.

On a more personal note, the standard definition of **self-condemnation** refers to an individual's act of judging, disapproving, or criticizing themselves, often for their actions, behavior, choices, or perceived shortcomings.

1. Self-Criticism: Self-condemnation involves harsh self-criticism or negative self-judgment. It can manifest as feelings of guilt, shame, or self-blame.

2. Internal Emotional State: It primarily represents an internal emotional state in which individuals are unforgiving or unkind to themselves, holding themselves to high standards or dwelling on perceived mistakes.

3. Psychological Impact: Self-condemnation can have a significant impact on an individual's mental and emotional well-being. It may lead to low self-esteem, anxiety, depression, and other mental health issues.

In summary, the standard definition of condemnation and self-condemnation revolves around societal and moral disapproval, often leading to social or legal consequences, while the biblical/spiritual definition focuses on divine judgment, eternal separation from God, and the potential for redemption through faith and belief in a higher power.

Biblical/Spiritual Definition of Condemnation and Self-Condemnation:

In 'The7Realms', **condemnation** takes on a different and more profound meaning in the words biblical and spiritual context:

1. Divine Judgment: Biblical condemnation refers to the idea of being judged by God for one's sins or moral transgressions. It is associated with the concept of divine justice and accountability for one's actions.

2. Eternal Separation: In a spiritual sense, condemnation implies a state of being separated from God because of one's sins. It signifies being "condemned" to an eternity apart from God, which is often associated with spiritual death or punishment.

3. Redemption and Salvation: The concept of condemnation in the Bible is closely linked to the idea of salvation and redemption through faith. For example, in Christianity, the belief in Jesus Christ is often seen as a means of escaping condemnation and achieving eternal life.

In a biblical or spiritual context of 'The7Realms', **self-condemnation** takes on a different dimension:

1. Spiritual Guilt: Self-condemnation is often associated with a deep sense of spiritual guilt or conviction. It reflects an individual's awareness of their own sinfulness and unworthiness before God.

2. Repentance and Redemption: Self-condemnation, in a spiritual context, can be a crucial step toward repentance and seeking God's forgiveness and redemption. It signifies a recognition of one's need for spiritual healing and transformation.

3. Grace and Forgiveness: The concept of self-condemnation in spirituality emphasizes the importance of God's grace and forgiveness. It encourages individuals to turn to God, seek forgiveness, and believe in the possibility of spiritual renewal and transformation.

A relevant biblical passage related to self-condemnation is Romans 8:1 (NIV): "Therefore, there is now no condemnation for those who are in Christ Jesus." This verse underscores the idea that those who have a relationship with Christ and seek forgiveness are released from self-condemnation and the spiritual consequences of their sins.

In summary, self-condemnation, both in standard and biblical/spiritual contexts, involves self-judgment and self-criticism. In 'The7Realms', the spiritual dimension of self-condemnation is marked by the recognition of one's sinfulness, the potential for redemption through faith and forgiveness, and the emphasis on God's grace and mercy in the face of self-judgment and guilt.

Standard Definition of Fear:

In standard terms, "fear" is an emotional response to perceived threats or dangers. It can be rational or irrational and is primarily associated with self-preservation.

1. Emotional Response: Fear is a natural and instinctual emotional response to situations or stimuli that are perceived as threats or potential sources of harm.

2. Rational and Irrational Fears: Standard fear can be both rational, such as the fear of physical danger, and irrational, such as phobias or anxieties that do not have a clear basis in reality.

3. Adaptive Response: In many cases, standard fear serves as an adaptive response, helping individuals make quick decisions to protect themselves in dangerous situations.

Biblical/Spiritual Definition of Fear:

In a biblical or spiritual context, "fear" takes on a different dimension:

1. Reverence and Awe: In spirituality and the Bible, fear is often associated with reverence or awe toward God. It signifies acknowledging God's authority, power, and holiness.

2. Fear of the Lord: The phrase "fear of the Lord" is frequently used in the Bible, and it emphasizes not being afraid of God in a terrifying sense but having a deep respect and a sense of duty and devotion to God.

3. Wisdom and Understanding: The fear of the Lord is often linked to wisdom and understanding. Proverbs 9:10 (NIV) states, "The fear of the Lord is the beginning of wisdom, and knowledge of the Holy One is understanding." This biblical concept suggests that true wisdom begins with a deep respect for God.

In summary, the key difference between the standard and biblical/spiritual definitions of fear is in the nature of the fear itself. In standard fear, it's primarily an emotional response to perceived threats or dangers, while in a biblical or spiritual context, fear is more about reverence and awe toward God and can lead to wisdom and a deeper understanding of divine truths.

In 'The7Realms', the emphasis on fear must shift from anxiety, perceived danger, and personal self-preservation to acknowledging Gods higher power, His authority over all, and His holiness.

The Biblical Explanation of "Fear Not"

The phrase "fear not" or "do not be afraid" appears numerous times in the Bible, and its meaning is deeply rooted in the biblical and spiritual context. When the Bible encourages individuals with the words "fear not," it conveys several significant messages:

1. **Trust in God**: "Fear not" often signifies a call to place trust and faith in God. It reassures individuals that God is in control and can provide protection, guidance, and support in times of trouble.

2. **Divine Comfort**: The phrase is often used in situations where individuals are facing uncertainty, challenges, or danger. It is a reminder that God is a source of comfort and peace in the midst of adversity.

3. **Assurance of God's Presence**: "Fear not" emphasizes the presence of God. It reminds individuals that God is with them, offering a sense of companionship and divine assistance.

4. **Overcoming Anxiety**: The phrase is used to address anxiety and worry. It encourages individuals to let go of their fears and anxieties, knowing that God cares for them and can ease their concerns.

5. **Facing the Unknown**: It is often spoken to people facing the unknown or dealing with circumstances beyond their control. "Fear not" serves as an affirmation that God has a plan and purpose even in the face of the unknown.

6. **Conquering Spiritual Fears**: In a spiritual context, "fear not" can also apply to individuals who may fear God's judgment or condemnation due to sin. It reassures them of God's forgiveness and the possibility of redemption through faith in Jesus Christ.

Key Bible Verses with "Fear Not":

- **Isaiah 41:10 (NIV)**: "So do not fear, for I am with you; do not be dismayed, for I am your God. I will strengthen you and help you; I will uphold you with my righteous right hand."

- **Psalm 23:4 (NIV)**: "Even though I walk through the darkest valley, I will fear no evil, for you are with me; your rod and your staff, they comfort me."

- **Matthew 10:31 (NIV)**: "So don't be afraid; you are worth more than many sparrows."

"Fear not" in the Bible is a powerful message of trust, comfort, and divine presence. It encourages individuals to rely on God, find solace in His care, and overcome fear and anxiety, whether in facing life's challenges or seeking spiritual redemption.

Standard Definition of Worry:

The standard definition of "worry" is a state of anxiety or unease about potential future problems, often related to personal concerns or uncertainties:

1. **Emotional State**: Worry is primarily an internal emotional state characterized by apprehension, uneasiness, or nervousness about future events or outcomes.

2. **Rumination on Problems**: It involves mental and emotional rumination, where individuals repeatedly think about, dwell on, or anticipate negative outcomes or difficulties.

3. **Psychological Impact**: The act of worrying can have various psychological and emotional impacts, including stress, sleep disturbances, and impaired decision-making.

4. **Problem-Solving or Avoidance**: Worry can sometimes lead to problem-solving behaviors where individuals actively seek solutions to their concerns. However, in other cases, it may lead to avoidance behavior, where individuals try to escape or ignore their worries.

Biblical/Spiritual Definition of Worry:

In a biblical or spiritual context, the concept of worry also differs:

1. **Trust in God**: In spirituality, worry is often contrasted with trust in God. It conveys the idea that excessive worry can reflect a lack of trust in God's providence, care, and control over one's life and circumstances.

2. **Seeking God's Kingdom**: The Bible often encourages individuals not to worry but to seek first the Kingdom of God. For instance, in Matthew 6:31-33 (NIV), Jesus says, "So do not worry, saying, 'What shall we eat?' or 'What shall we drink?' or 'What shall we wear?' For the pagans run after all these things, and your heavenly Father knows that you need them. But seek first his kingdom and his righteousness, and all these things will be given to you as well." This teaching emphasizes prioritizing spiritual and moral values over material concerns.

3. **God's Care**: The spiritual perspective on worry reassures individuals that God knows their needs and cares for them. It encourages trust in God's provision and guidance.

In summary, while the standard definition of worry is primarily focused on personal anxiety and future uncertainties, the biblical/spiritual definition emphasizes the importance of trust in God, seeking spiritual values, and recognizing God's care and provision. It encourages individuals to shift their focus from excessive concern about worldly matters to a deeper reliance on faith and divine guidance.

Ryan C. Neal, MD

The Exercise- The Mindfulness and Meditation Practice for The Fifth Realm

Mindfulness Meditation for Rising Above Condemnation, Fear, and Worry

Certainly, mindfulness and meditation can be applied to the biblical concepts of condemnation, self-condemnation, fear, and worry as a means of fostering spiritual growth and well-being. Here's an outline of a mindfulness and meditation practice based on these concepts: (Spend at least 2-3 mins on each bullet point.)

The Fifth Realm- Mindfulness and Meditation- Preparation:

- Find a quiet and comfortable space where you can sit or lie down without distractions.
- Take a few deep breaths to calm your mind and relax your body.
- Begin by setting an intention for your practice. This can be a desire to deepen your understanding of these biblical concepts, find inner peace, or seek spiritual guidance.

The Fifth Realm- Mindfulness and Meditation- Contemplating Condemnation:

- Focus on the concept of condemnation as presented in the Bible. Consider instances where condemnation is discussed and its implications.
- Reflect on your own experiences with judgment and criticism. Have you ever felt condemned or condemned others? How did it affect you or them?
- Practice non-judgmental awareness, acknowledging your thoughts and feelings without self-condemnation.

The Fifth Realm- Mindfulness and Meditation- Contemplating Self-Condemnation:

- Explore the concept of self-condemnation in a biblical context. Reflect on any moments in your life where you've been harsh on yourself or felt unworthy.
- Consider the possibility of self-forgiveness and redemption through faith. Reflect on the idea that God's grace can offer forgiveness and healing.
- Practice self-compassion by offering yourself the same kindness and forgiveness you believe God extends to you.

The Fifth Realm- Mindfulness and Meditation- Contemplating the Concept of Fear:

- Shift your focus to the concept of fear as found in the Bible. Consider biblical passages that address fear, awe, and reverence of God.
- Explore your own fears, both rational and irrational, and how they may impact your spiritual journey.
- Embrace the idea of "fear of the Lord" as a form of reverence and awe, acknowledging God's power and wisdom.

Mindfulness Meditation for Rising Above Condemnation, Fear, and Worry

The Fifth Realm- Mindfulness and Meditation- Contemplating Worry:

- Reflect on biblical teachings about worry and anxiety. Explore verses that encourage trust in God's provision and care.

- Examine your own worries and anxieties, especially those related to worldly concerns. Consider how excessive worry might hinder your spiritual growth.

- Embrace the concept of seeking God's kingdom and righteousness as a way to prioritize spiritual values over material worries.

The Fifth Realm- Mindfulness and Meditation Practice:

- Begin a meditation practice by focusing on your breath. Pay attention to each inhale and exhale, allowing your mind to settle.

- When thoughts related to condemnation, self-condemnation, fear, or worry arise, acknowledge them without judgment, and gently return your focus to your breath.

- Practice mindfulness by staying present in the moment, letting go of past judgments and future anxieties.

The Fifth Realm- Mindfulness and Meditation- Closing and Reflection:

- Gradually bring your meditation to a close. Take a few deep breaths and open your eyes. Reflect on the insights and emotions that arose during your practice.

- Consider how you can apply these biblical concepts and the mindfulness practice to your daily life.

- Express gratitude for the opportunity to engage with these concepts and work toward greater spiritual peace and understanding.

The 'The7Realms' mindfulness and meditation practice can help you deepen your understanding of biblical concepts while fostering inner peace, self-compassion, and trust in God's guidance. It can be a valuable tool for personal and spiritual growth.

Questions for Week 8/Lesson 8

[Remember to practice **The Mindfulness and Meditation Exercise** associated with this lesson *after completing each daily question*.]

Week 8: Day 1

Contemplate the concept of **'Condemnation, Fear, and Worry'** (the first realm of lower spiritual consciousness- spiritual unwellness) as it relates 'The7Realms'. What do these subconsciousness feelings mean to you and your well-beingness?

_____
_____
_____
_____
_____
_____
_____
_____
_____
_____
_____
_____
_____
_____
_____
_____

Week 8: Day 2

Contemplate the meaning/concept of the word- **Condemnation**. What are some of the differences between the standard definition and biblical definition of Condemnation?

_____
_____
_____
_____
_____
_____
_____
_____
_____
_____
_____
_____
_____
_____
_____
_____
_____

Week 8: Day 3

Contemplate the meaning/concept of the word- **Fear**. What are some of the differences between the standard definition and biblical definition of Fear?

Week 8: Day 4

Contemplate the meaning/concept of the word- **Worry**. What are some of the differences between the standard definition and biblical definition of Worry?

Week 8: Day 5

Contemplate the **Realm of Condemnation, Fear and Worry**. How might the negative Thoughts, Feelings, and Emotions of Condemnation, Fear, and Worry, have a **negative synergistic effect** on your Spiritual Consciousness?

_____
_____
_____
_____
_____
_____
_____
_____
_____
_____
_____
_____
_____
_____
_____
_____

Week 8: Day 6

What would it mean to you could transcend these Lower Spiritual Consciousness thoughts and be able to **live a greater percentage of your conscious life** in Higher Spiritual Consciousness Realms?

_____
_____
_____
_____
_____
_____
_____
_____
_____
_____
_____
_____
_____
_____
_____
_____
_____
_____

Week 8: Day 7

How do you think **your spiritual well-being would be improved** spending more time in the Higher Spiritual Consciousness? How do you think **your physical well-being might be improved**?

Week 9/Lesson 9: The Sixth Realm- Unforgiveness, Anger, and Doubt

Lesson 9: The Sixth Realm- Unforgiveness, Anger, and Doubt

9.1- The Sixth Trilateral Realm- The Realm of Unforgiveness, Anger, and Doubt

9.2- The Corresponding Scriptures for The Realm of Unforgiveness, Anger, and Doubt

9.3- Understanding the Concepts of Unforgiveness, Anger, and Doubt in 'The7Realms'

9.4- Contemplating the Biblical and Spiritual Concepts of Unforgiveness, Anger, and Doubt

The Exercise- The Mindfulness and Meditation Practice of The Sixth Realm

Questions for Week 9/Lesson 9

9.1- The Sixth Trilateral Realm
The Realm of **Unforgiveness, Anger, and Doubt**
"But now you yourselves are to put off all these: anger, wrath, malice, blasphemy, filthy language out of your mouth."

Ryan C. Neal, MD

The Structure and Organization of The Seven Realms of Spiritual Consciousness

The Seven Trilateral Realms of **The Pyramid of Sovereignty**:

The First *Trilateral* **Realm of Spiritual Consciousness**

- The Realm of The Trinity- God the Father, God the Son, and God the Holy Spirit

The Second *Trilateral* **Realm of Spiritual Consciousness**

- The Realm of Love, Peace, and Joy- The Realm of "Fruit of The Spirit"

The Third *Trilateral* **Realm of Spiritual Consciousness**

- The Realm of Ask, Seek and Knock-The Realms of Manifestation

The Fourth *Trilateral* **Realm of Spiritual Consciousness**

- The Realm of Mind, Body, and Soul (MBS)- The Mental, The Physical and The Spiritual

The Fifth *Trilateral* **Realm of Spiritual Consciousness**

- The Realm of Self-Condemnation, Fear and Worry

The Sixth *Trilateral* Realm of Spiritual Consciousness

- The Realm of Unforgiveness (Hatred), Anger and Doubt

The Seventh *Trilateral* **Realm of Spiritual Consciousness**

- The Realm of Internal Disease, External Disease, and Mental and Psychological Disease- The Realm of Disease Manifestation

The Sixth Trilateral Realm- *The Realm of **Unforgiveness, Anger and Doubt***

The **Sixth** *Trilateral* Realm of Spiritual Consciousness is the **Realm of Unforgiveness (Hatred), Anger, and Doubt (UAD).**

This realm represents *the progression of negative subconscious thoughts* that evolve from *the negative spiritual energy* that exists in The *Fifth Realm of Condemnation, Fear and Doubt.*

This evolution of *un*wellness is the beginning of the **physical manifestation of disease or *'dis-ease'*.**

9.2- The Corresponding Scriptures for The Realm of Unforgiveness, Anger, and Doubt

The Corresponding Scriptures of Unforgiveness, Anger, and Doubt

Matthew 6:12-15 (KJV)

12 And forgive us our debts, as we forgive our debtors.

13 And lead us not into temptation but deliver us from evil: For thine is the kingdom, and the power, and the glory, forever. Amen.

14 For if ye forgive men their trespasses, your heavenly Father will also forgive you:

15 But if ye forgive not men their trespasses, neither will your Father forgive your trespasses.

Colossians 3:8-11 (NKJV)

8 But now you yourselves are to put off all these: anger, wrath, malice, blasphemy, filthy language out of your mouth. 9 Do not lie to one another, since you have put off the old man with his deeds, 10 and have put on the new man who is renewed in knowledge according to the image of Him who created him, 11 where there is neither Greek nor Jew, circumcised nor uncircumcised, barbarian, Scythian, slave nor free, but Christ is all and in all.

Mark 11:23 (NKJV)

23 For assuredly, I say to you, whoever says to this mountain, 'Be removed and be cast into the sea,' *and does not doubt in his heart, but believes that those things he says will be done, he will have whatever he says.*

9.3- Understanding the Concepts of Unforgiveness, Anger, and Doubt in 'The7Realms'

The Realm of Unforgiveness, Anger, and Doubt

The Sixth Realm is the Realm of Unforgiveness (Hate), Anger, and Doubt (UAD). This is the realm where the manifestation of self-condemnation comes to life as hatred and or unforgiveness. Even if this unforgiveness is of self.

Unforgiveness- The Bible is very clear on forgiveness and even goes so far as to say that he who does not forgive his brother will not be forgiven by God.

Forgiveness is at the pinnacle of spiritual enlightenment and spiritual growth. **Unforgiveness, much like hatred, blocks our ability to progress to higher consciousness and condemns us to dwell in lower consciousness states.**

Hate- The Bible is very clear on its direction for us not to hate. We are not to hate our brothers, we are not to hate ourselves, we are not to hate God, but instead we are to love one another as God loved us.

Anger- In this realm, the spirit of fear and anxiety can manifest as anger. Anger being the physical manifestation of fear and anxiety whether it be related to the past, present or future stressors, perceived threats, or trauma.

Doubt- The Bible says do not doubt just as it says do not worry. The Bible understands that worry will lead to doubt and God cannot bless a doubtful mind. **In the Sixth Realm the transition from worry (in the Fifth Realm) begins to solidify as a belief and becomes doubt.** I perceive doubt as being a much more substantive extension of worry.

The trilateral realm of **Unforgiveness (Hate), Anger, and Doubt** causes you to transition further into lower spiritual consciousness from the realm of **Condemnation, Fear, and Worry**.

The extension of **unforgiving, angry, and doubtful thoughts, feelings, and emotions** causes us to transition further into **spiritual entropy** and begins **to manifest as physical, mental, and psychological diseases.**

In 'The7Realms', the act of being mindful of **love, peace and joy** allows us to focus beyond the lower spiritual realm of **condemnation, fear and worry** and prevents us from **the carnal descent** into the spiritual entropy of **unforgiveness, anger, and doubt.**

9.4- Contemplating the Biblical and Spiritual Concepts of Unforgiveness, Anger, and Doubt

Unforgiveness in The Sixth Realm

Unforgiveness is a deeply rooted emotional state characterized by the persistent refusal or inability to let go of resentment, anger, or a desire for retribution toward someone who has wronged you.

It involves the unwillingness to grant the transgressor absolution or to release the emotional burdens associated with the past offense. Unforgiveness can lead to ongoing emotional pain and can hinder personal growth and the potential for reconciliation or healing in relationships.

Unforgiveness is a sin. It blocks our ability to clearly hear Gods voice and thus His will for your life.

The simple answer to unforgiveness is forgiveness. But this is sometimes easier said than done. Forgiveness often requires a significant amount of spiritual energy and courage depending on the degree of offense to be forgiven.

In the Bible, the response to unforgiveness is rooted in several key principles and teachings, primarily found in the teachings of Jesus and other biblical passages. Here are some of the central aspects of the biblical response to unforgiveness:

1. **Forgiveness is a Command:** The Bible emphasizes forgiveness as a fundamental Christian duty. In Matthew 6:14-15 (NIV), Jesus says, "For if you forgive other people when they sin against you, your heavenly Father will also forgive you. But if you do not forgive others their sins, your Father will not forgive your sins." This underscores the importance of forgiveness in the Christian faith.

2. **Forgive as You've Been Forgiven:** Christians are encouraged to forgive others as God has forgiven them. Ephesians 4:32 (NIV) says, "Be kind and compassionate to one another, forgiving each other, just as in Christ God forgave you." This means extending the same grace and mercy that one has received from God to others.

3. **Reconciliation and Restoration:** The Bible promotes reconciliation and restoration of relationships where possible. In Matthew 5:23-24 (NIV), Jesus advises reconciling with a brother before offering gifts at the altar, emphasizing the importance of resolving conflicts.

4. **Letting Go of Bitterness:** Hebrews 12:15 (NIV) warns against allowing a "root of bitterness" to take hold, as it can defile and harm many. Forgiveness helps in uprooting bitterness and resentment.

5. **Prayer and Love for Enemies:** Jesus teaches in Matthew 5:44 (NIV), "But I tell you, love your enemies and pray for those who persecute you." This approach reflects the idea of responding to hurt with love and prayer, ultimately working toward forgiveness.

6. **Forgiving Seventy Times Seven:** In Matthew 18:21-22 (NIV), Jesus tells Peter that forgiveness should be limitless, suggesting that forgiveness should not have a set limit but should be offered continually.

7. **Seeking Forgiveness:** The Bible also encourages us to seek forgiveness when we have wronged others. In Matthew 5:23-24, Jesus advises reconciling with someone who has something against you.

In summary, the biblical response to unforgiveness is one of extending forgiveness, seeking reconciliation, and showing love, grace, and mercy, as modeled by the forgiveness God offers to humanity through Christ. It's not only a command but also a path to personal healing and restoration of relationships.

Hate/Hatred in The Sixth Realm

Hatred is a sin. Hate is defined as an intense or passionate dislike or disdain for something or someone. The definition of hate from standard, spiritual, and biblical perspectives:

Standard Definition: Hate is an intense and profound feeling of aversion, hostility, or extreme dislike toward someone or something, often accompanied by negative emotions, a desire for harm, or a wish for their suffering or removal.

Spiritual Perspective: In a spiritual context, hate is a harmful and negative emotional state that reflects a disconnection from divine love and compassion. It is viewed as a destructive force that separates individuals from their higher spiritual selves and disrupts harmonious relationships with others.

Biblical Perspective: According to the Bible, hate is a sinful and morally reprehensible attitude or emotion. It is often associated with harboring resentment, bearing grudges, and wishing ill upon others. In contrast to the biblical command to love one's neighbor and even one's enemies, hate is seen as incompatible with the principles of love, forgiveness, and reconciliation taught in the Bible. It is considered a spiritual and moral transgression that hinders one's relationship with God and others.

Unforgiveness and Hate in The Sixth Realm

Unforgiveness and hate are closely related from a spiritual and biblical perspective, and both are viewed negatively in the teachings of the Bible. Here's how they are connected:

1. **Unforgiveness Leads to Hate:** Unforgiveness often festers and grows into bitterness and hatred. When a person holds onto grudges, resentment, and a desire for revenge, it can eventually transform into a deep-seated hatred towards the person who wronged them. In Matthew 18:35 (NIV), Jesus speaks of an unforgiving servant who was handed over to jailers until he could pay his debt, emphasizing the harmful consequences of unforgiveness.

2. **Hate as a Sin:** Hate is considered a sin in many biblical passages. For example, in 1 John 3:15 (NIV), it is stated, "Anyone who hates a brother or sister is a murderer, and you know that no murderer has eternal life residing in him." This verse underscores the seriousness of harboring hate in one's heart.

3. **Love Your Enemies:** The Bible teaches the importance of loving one's enemies and those who wrong you. In Matthew 5:44 (NIV), Jesus says, "But I tell you, love your enemies and pray for those who persecute you." This command directly opposes the cultivation of hate and encourages forgiveness instead.

4. **Forgiveness as a Remedy:** Unforgiveness and hate can be counteracted through forgiveness. By forgiving those who have wronged us, we are following the biblical command to extend grace, mercy, and love. Forgiveness is a means to release the negative emotions associated with unforgiveness and hate.

5. **Freedom in Forgiveness:** Forgiveness is also seen as a path to personal freedom and spiritual well-being. When we forgive, we free ourselves from the burdens of hate and resentment. Colossians 3:13 (NIV) encourages forgiveness, stating, "Bear with each other and forgive one another if any of you has a grievance against someone. Forgive as the Lord forgave you."

In essence, unforgiveness and hate are interconnected in that unforgiveness often leads to hate, and both are discouraged in the Bible. Instead, the biblical perspective emphasizes forgiveness, love, and reconciliation as the path to healing, inner peace, and spiritual growth. It encourages individuals to let go of the negative emotions associated with unforgiveness and hatred, promoting a more loving and compassionate approach to conflicts and grievances.

Anger in The Sixth Realm

Standard Definition: Anger is a powerful and intense emotional response characterized by a heightened state of arousal, often triggered by perceived injustice, frustration, or opposition. It manifests in various degrees, from mild irritation to intense fury, and can lead to physiological, cognitive, and behavioral changes.

Spiritual Perspective: In a spiritual context, anger is recognized as a natural human emotion but is seen as a potential obstacle to spiritual growth. It is often associated with ego, attachment, and a lack of inner peace. Spiritual teachings emphasize the importance of transforming anger into constructive responses, fostering compassion, and maintaining inner harmony.

Biblical Perspective: The Bible acknowledges the existence of anger. Ephesians 4:26-27 (NIV) advises, "In your anger, do not sin: Do not let the sun go down while you are still angry, and do not give the devil a foothold." This suggests that while anger may arise, it should be managed without leading to sin or prolonged bitterness. Additionally, Proverbs 14:29 (NIV) states, "Whoever is patient has great understanding, but one who is quick-tempered displays folly," emphasizing the value of patience over quick, uncontrolled anger. Biblical teachings highlight the importance of forgiveness and reconciliation over harboring anger and resentment.

Doubt in The Sixth Realm

Standard Definition: Doubt is a state of uncertainty or hesitation regarding the truth, validity, or reliability of something. Even worse is self-doubt- the doubting of one's own value or worth.

Spiritual Perspective: In a spiritual context, doubt is the wavering of faith or trust in the divine, higher power, or spiritual truths. It can manifest as uncertainty about the existence of the divine, the efficacy of spiritual practices, or the meaning and purpose of life. Overcoming doubt in a spiritual context often involves a deepening of faith, seeking understanding, and cultivating a connection with the transcendent.

Biblical Perspective: The Bible addresses doubt, recognizing it as a human experience. In James 1:6-8 (NIV), it is written, "But when you ask, you must believe and not doubt, because the one who doubts is like a wave of the sea, blown and tossed by the wind. That person should not expect to receive anything from the Lord. Such a person is double-minded and unstable in all they do." This suggests that doubt can hinder the efficacy of prayer and spiritual growth. However, the Bible also portrays instances of individuals expressing doubt, and in those cases, seeking understanding and guidance is encouraged. Doubt becomes problematic when it leads to a persistent lack of trust or faith without a willingness to seek resolution.

The Exercise- The Mindfulness and Meditation Practice of The Sixth Realm

Mindfulness and Meditation Practice for The Sixth Realm

Mindfulness and meditation can be powerful tools for addressing biblical concepts of 'The7Realms' such as *unforgiveness, hate, anger, and doubt.* Here's an outline for a practice that integrates these principles: (Spend at least 2-3 mins on each bullet point.)

The Sixth Realm- Mindfulness and Meditation- Setting the Intentions:

- Begin by acknowledging your intention for this practice, which is to cultivate a spirit of forgiveness, love, patience, and faith in alignment with biblical principles.

The Sixth Realm- Mindfulness and Meditation- Breath Awareness:

- Find a comfortable and quiet space.
- Close your eyes and focus on your breath.
- Inhale deeply, exhale slowly. Be fully present with each breath.
- As you breathe, release tension, and clear your mind.

The Sixth Realm- Mindfulness and Meditation- Forgiveness Meditation:

- Visualize a person or situation causing unforgiveness.
- Acknowledge the pain but choose to release it.
- Repeat a forgiveness mantra, such as "I choose to forgive and let go."
- Envision a sense of lightness and peace as you release unforgiveness.

The Sixth Realm- Mindfulness and Meditation- Love and Compassion Reflection:

- Contemplate biblical teachings on love, such as 1 Corinthians 13.
- Reflect on ways to express love and compassion towards others.
- Consider specific actions you can take to demonstrate love.

The Sixth Realm- Mindfulness and Meditation- Anger Transformation:

- Identify sources of anger in your life.
- Breathe deeply, allowing the breath to diffuse anger.
- Visualize transforming anger into constructive energy.
- Reflect on Ephesians 4:26-27 and commit to managing anger wisely.

Mindfulness and Meditation Practice for The Sixth Realm

The Sixth Realm- Mindfulness and Meditation- Doubt Reflection:
- Acknowledge any doubts you may have in your faith.
- Journal about specific doubts or uncertainties.
- Explore relevant Bible verses addressing doubt (e.g., Mark 9:24, James 1:6-8).
- Affirm your faith and seek understanding through prayer.

The Sixth Realm- Mindfulness and Meditation- Gratitude and Faith Cultivation:
- Shift your focus to gratitude for the positive aspects of your life.
- Contemplate biblical verses on faith (e.g., Hebrews 11:1).
- Affirm your trust in divine wisdom and timing.

The Sixth Realm- Mindfulness and Meditation- Closing and Reflection:
- Gradually bring your awareness back to the present moment.
- Express gratitude for the insights gained during the practice.
- Consider ways to integrate these principles into your daily life.

This practice aims to integrate mindfulness and biblical principles, fostering a deeper understanding and embodiment of forgiveness, love, patience, and faith.

Questions for Week 9/Lesson 9

[Remember to practice **The Mindfulness and Meditation Exercise** associated with this lesson *after completing each daily question*.]

Week 9: Day 1

Contemplate the concept of **'Unforgiveness (Hatred), Anger, and Doubt'** (the second realm of lower spiritual consciousness- spiritual unwellness) as it relates 'The7Realms'. What might these subconsciousness emotions mean to you and your well-beingness?

_____
_____
_____
_____
_____
_____
_____
_____
_____
_____
_____
_____
_____
_____
_____
_____
_____

Week 9: Day 2

Contemplate the meaning/concept of the word- **Unforgiveness**. What are some of the differences between the standard definition and biblical definition of Condemnation? How are the concepts of unforgiveness and hate interrelated?

Week 9: Day 3

Contemplate the meaning/concept of the word- **Anger.** What are some of the differences between the standard definition and biblical definition of Anger?

Week 9: Day 4

Contemplate the meaning/concept of the word- **Doubt**. What are some of the differences between the standard definition and biblical definition of Doubt?

Week 9: Day 5

Contemplate the **Realm of Unforgiveness (Hatred), Anger, and Doubt.** How might the negative Thoughts, Feelings, and Emotions of Unforgiveness (Hatred), Anger, and Doubt, have a **negative synergistic effect** on your Spiritual Consciousness?

_____
_____
_____
_____
_____
_____
_____
_____
_____
_____
_____
_____
_____
_____
_____
_____
_____

Week 9: Day 6

What would it mean to you could transcend these Lower Spiritual Consciousness thoughts and be able to **live a greater percentage of your conscious life** in Higher Spiritual Consciousness Realms?

Week 9: Day 7

How do you think **your spiritual well-being would be improved** spending more time in the Higher Spiritual Consciousness? How do you think **your physical well-being might be improved**?

Week 10/ Lesson 10: The Seventh Realm- Disease Manifestation

Week 10/ Lesson 10: The Seventh Realm- Disease Manifestation

10.1- The Seventh Trilateral Realm- The Realm of Internal, External, and Mental/Psychological Diseases

10.2- The Corresponding Scriptures for The Realm of Internal, External, and Mental/Psychological Diseases

10.3- Understanding the Concepts of Internal, External, and Mental/Psychological Diseases in 'The7Realms'

10.4- Contemplating the Biblical and Spiritual Concepts of Internal, External, and Mental Diseases

The Exercise- The Mindfulness and Meditation Practice for The Seventh Realm

Questions for Week 10/Lesson 10

10.1- The Seventh Trilateral Realm
The Realm of **Internal, External, and Mental/Psychological Diseases**

"And He said to her, "Daughter, your faith has made you well. Go in peace and be healed of your affliction."

The Gift of 'The7Realms'

The Structure and Organization of The Seven Realms of Spiritual Consciousness

The Seven Trilateral Realms of **The Pyramid of Sovereignty:**

The First *Trilateral* **Realm of Spiritual Consciousness**

- The Realm of The Trinity- God the Father, God the Son, and God the Holy Spirit

The Second *Trilateral* **Realm of Spiritual Consciousness**

- The Realm of Love, Peace, and Joy- The Realm of "Fruit of The Spirit"

The Third *Trilateral* **Realm of Spiritual Consciousness**

- The Realm of Ask, Seek and Knock-The Realms of Manifestation

The Fourth *Trilateral* **Realm of Spiritual Consciousness**

- The Realm of Mind, Body, and Soul (MBS)- The Mental, The Physical and The Spiritual

The Fifth *Trilateral* **Realm of Spiritual Consciousness**

- The Realm of Self-Condemnation, Fear and Worry

The Sixth *Trilateral* **Realm of Spiritual Consciousness**

- The Realm of Unforgiveness (Hatred), Anger and Doubt

The Seventh *Trilateral* Realm of Spiritual Consciousness

- The Realm of Internal Disease, External Disease, and Mental and Psychological Disease- The Realm of Disease Manifestation

The Seventh Trilateral Realm- *The Realm of **Internal, External and Mental Diseases***

The Seventh *Trilateral* Realm of Spiritual Consciousness is the Realm of Internal Diseases, External Diseases, and Mental and Psychological Diseases (IEP).

This is the realm of *un*wellness where the culmination of the **negative spiritual energy (Fifth Realm)** combines with the **negative spiritual and physical energy (Sixth Realm)** to *create* the manifestation of physical disease.

Without *conscious attention* (mindfulness) and *directed intention* (meditation), your mind subconsciously descends through the 5th and 6th Realms of Spiritual Consciousness and falls prey to disease manifestation (Internal, External, and Psychological Diseases).

10.2- The Corresponding Scriptures for The Realm of Internal, External, and Mental/Psychological Diseases

The Corresponding Scriptures of Internal, External, and Psychological Disease

James 1: 12-15 (NKJV) Loving God Under Trials

*¹² Blessed is the man who endures temptation; for when he has been approved, he will receive the crown of life which the Lord has promised to those who love Him. ¹³ Let no one say when he is tempted, "I am tempted by God"; for God cannot be tempted by evil, nor does He Himself tempt anyone. **¹⁴ But each one is tempted when he is drawn away by his own desires and enticed. ¹⁵ Then, when desire has conceived, it gives birth to sin; and sin, when it is full-grown, brings forth death.***

Matthew 9:28 (NKJV)

*²⁸ And when He had come into the house, **the blind men came to Him. And Jesus said to them, "Do you believe that I am able to do this?" They said to Him, "Yes, Lord."***

Mark 5:25-34 (NKJV)

*²⁵ Now a certain woman had a flow of blood for twelve years, ²⁶ and had suffered many things from many physicians. She had spent all that she had and was no better, but rather grew worse. ²⁷ When she heard about Jesus, she came behind Him in the crowd and touched His garment. ²⁸ **For she said, "If only I may touch His clothes, I shall be made well."***

²⁹ Immediately the fountain of her blood was dried up, and she felt in her body that she was healed of the [f]affliction. *³⁰ And Jesus, immediately knowing in Himself that power had gone out of Him, turned around in the crowd and said, "Who touched My clothes?"*

³¹ But His disciples said to Him, "You see the multitude thronging You, and You say, 'Who touched Me?'

*³² And He looked around to see her who had done this thing. ³³ But the woman, fearing and trembling, knowing what had happened to her, came and fell down before Him and told Him the whole truth. **³⁴ And He said to her, "Daughter, your faith has made you well. Go in peace and be healed of your affliction.***

The Corresponding Scriptures of Internal, External, and Psychological Disease

Matthew 8:1-3 (NKJV) Jesus Cleanses a Leper

8 When He had come down from the mountain, great multitudes followed Him. ***2 And behold, a leper came and worshiped Him, saying, "Lord, if You are willing, You can make me clean."***

3 Then Jesus put out His hand and touched him, saying, "I am willing; be cleansed." Immediately his leprosy was cleansed.

4 And Jesus said to him, "See that you tell no one; but go your way, show yourself to the priest, and offer the gift that Moses commanded, as a testimony to them.

Matthew 12: 22-30 (NKJV)- *A House Divided Cannot Stand*

22 Then one was brought to Him who was demon-possessed, blind and mute; and He healed him, so that the [d]blind and mute man both spoke and saw. *23 And all the multitudes were amazed and said, "Could this be the Son of David?"*

24 Now when the Pharisees heard it they said, "This fellow does not cast out demons except by [e]Beelzebub, the ruler of the demons."

25 But Jesus knew their thoughts and said to them: "Every kingdom divided against itself is brought to desolation, and every city or house divided against itself will not stand. 26 If Satan casts out Satan, he is divided against himself. How then will his kingdom stand? 27 And if I cast out demons by Beelzebub, by whom do your sons cast them out? Therefore, they shall be your judges.

28 But if I cast out demons by the Spirit of God, surely the kingdom of God has come upon you. *29 Or how can one enter a strong man's house and plunder his goods, unless he first binds the strong man? And then he will plunder his house. 30 He, who is not with Me, is against Me, and he who does not gather with Me scatters abroad.*

10.3- Understanding the Concepts of Internal, External, and Mental/Psychological Diseases in 'The7Realms'

The Seventh Trilateral Realm- The Realm of Internal, External and Mental Diseases

The Realm of Internal, External, and Mental and Psychological Diseases

As spiritual beings having a physical experience, it is vitally important to understand the essence of how spiritual unwellness equates to physical unwellness. The Seven Trilateral Realms of Spiritual Consciousness outlines how easy it is for your Thoughts, Feelings, and Emotions (TFEs) to descend into physical unwellness, or worse physical disease.

Higher Consciousness = Spiritual Wellness

⬇

Spiritual Entropy

(subconscious negative thoughts)

⬇

Lower Consciousness = Spiritual Unwellness

By dwelling or unknowingly spending too much time in negative spiritual energy (negative TFEs) our spiritual beingness becomes physically unwell when our innermost thoughts are unwell.

As a practicing physician for more than 25 years, I became aware that many of our physical ailments do not simply emanate from physical disorders alone but instead often evolve from spiritual disorders.

Spiritual Unwellness and Spiritual Entropy

This spiritual disorder (spiritual entropy) occurs when we allow our Mind, Body, and Soul (MBS- The 4th Realm) to descend into negative subconscious Thoughts, Feelings, and Emotions (TFEs) and exert a harmful effect upon our physical well-being.

The Seventh Realm of Spiritual Consciousness (The 7th Realm) is the culmination of unintended **spiritual entropy** that occurs from *inattention* to conscious mindfulness in the face of everyday stressors.

Without *conscious attention* (mindfulness) and *directed intention* (prayer-meditation), your mind subconsciously descends through the 5th and 6th Realms of Spiritual Consciousness and falls prey to disease manifestation (Internal, External, and Psychological Diseases).

The Seventh Trilateral Realm- The Realm of Internal, External and Mental Diseases

The Descent through Spiritual Entropy- The 5th and 6th Realms of Spiritual Consciousness

In 'The7realms', the unwell Thoughts, Feelings, and Emotions (TFEs) of the subconscious began in the 5th and 6th Realm. The Realm of Condemnation (lack of self-love), Fear, and Worry (The 5th Realm) and The Realm of Unforgiveness (Hatred), Anger, and Doubt (The 6th Realm).

The 5th Realm- The Realm of Condemnation, Fear, and Worry

⬇

The 6th Realm- The Realm of Unforgiveness, Anger, and Doubt

⬇

The 7th Realm- The Realm of Internal, External, and Psychological Diseases

The negative TFEs of the 5th and 6th Realms lead to negative neuronal (Thoughts), hormonal (Feelings), and chemical (Emotions) reactions within the body which began to distort the physiological inscription into the subconscious mind and subsequently initiate the spiritual process of disease manifestation within your physical beingness.

The Bible and Internal, External, and Psychological Disease

Of note, the Bible speaks of many kinds of disease and disease states. For example, internal disease is described by things such as blindness, deafness, and the woman with the issue of blood. External diseases in the Bible are depicted with things such as leprosy, deformities, and paralysis. Mental and psychological diseases are labelled as 'madness' (out-of-the-mind states), fits and seizures, and even demonic possessions.

In truth, the manifestation of disease is incredibly complex and involves physiologic, genetic, environmental, and psychosocial determinants.

However, the root cause of such disease is often related to the lack of awareness of the subconscious physiological effects of negative TFEs deeply rooted in the subconscious mind.

The consistent application of the Mindfulness and Meditation practices of 'The7Realms' can help to override those subconscious TFEs, reprogram your subconscious mind, and redirect your spiritual energy to spend more time in your Higher Spiritual Consciousness, thereby reducing your predisposition to spiritual unwellness leading to physical unwellness.

The Seventh Trilateral Realm- The Realm of Internal, External and Mental Diseases

Internal diseases, external diseases, and mental and psychological diseases represent distinct categories of health conditions, each with its unique characteristics and impact on the body.

Internal Diseases:

- Definition: Internal diseases, often referred to as medical or physical diseases, affect the internal structures and organs of the body.

- Causes: These diseases can result from genetic factors, infections, autoimmune responses, metabolic disorders, or lifestyle choices.

- Manifestations: Symptoms are often observable and measurable, such as pain, inflammation, changes in organ function, or abnormalities in laboratory tests.

- Examples: Cardiovascular diseases, cancer, respiratory disorders, gastrointestinal conditions, and endocrine disorders are examples of internal diseases.

External Diseases:

- Definition: One example of external diseases are things that enter the body from an outside (external) source, such as infectious or communicable diseases. These diseases are caused by pathogens such as bacteria, viruses, parasites, or fungi and can be transmitted from one person to another.

- Causes: Transmission occurs through contact with contaminated surfaces, air, and even bodily fluids.

- Manifestations: Symptoms may include fever, rash, cough, and other signs of infection.

- Examples: Influenza, tuberculosis- leprosy and malaria are examples of external diseases.

The Seventh Trilateral Realm- The Realm of Internal, External and Mental Diseases

Mental and Psychological Diseases:

- Definition: Mental and psychological diseases, also known as mental health disorders, affect cognitive, emotional, and behavioral aspects of an individual.

- Causes: Factors include genetic predisposition, brain chemistry, trauma, and environmental stressors.

- Manifestations: Symptoms often involve disturbances in mood, thought processes, or behavior, impacting social functioning and daily life.

- Examples: Depression, anxiety disorders, schizophrenia, and bipolar disorder fall into the category of mental and psychological diseases.

Comparison:

- All three types of diseases can have a significant impact on overall health and well-being.

- They may share common risk factors, such as genetics, lifestyle, and environmental influences.

Contrast:

- Internal diseases primarily affect physical structures and organ systems, whereas mental and psychological diseases primarily affect cognitive and emotional functions.

- External diseases are characterized by being contagious and often involve the transmission of pathogens, unlike internal and mental diseases.

- Internal and external diseases typically have more observable physical symptoms, whereas mental and psychological diseases may present with subtler signs that are often internalized and subjective.

While internal and external diseases primarily affect the physical body, mental and psychological diseases focus on the intricate interplay of thoughts, emotions, and behavior. Each category requires unique approaches to diagnosis, treatment, and prevention.

My Physician Statement

As a physician, I am keenly aware of the physical, genetic, environmental, and psychosocial factors that contribute to physical illness.

It is paramount to stress that I am a staunch advocate for appropriate medical management across all disease categories.

Nothing in this workbook should replace the recommendations and treatments provided by your personal physicians.

However, addressing only the physical aspects of illness without considering spiritual needs is not the most effective approach. A complementary and holistic approach is always preferred.

As a student of Spiritual Consciousness, Christian Mindfulness, and Biblical Meditation, I have recognized the positive impact of mindfulness and meditation in managing disease.

Through the principles outlined in 'The7Realms', I have discovered a method to alleviate much of the pain and suffering associated with physical illness and the negative spiritual consciousness that contributes to unwell thoughts, feelings, and emotions.

I share these insights in The Gift of 'The7Realms'.

-R.C. Neal, MD

10.4- Contemplating the Biblical and Spiritual Concepts of Internal, External, and Mental Diseases

Contemplating the Biblical and Spiritual Concepts of Internal, External, and Mental Diseases

Physical Disease in The Seventh Realm

Physical disease refers to a pathological condition that adversely affects the normal functioning of the body's structures or organs, leading to observable and often measurable abnormalities in physical health. These conditions result from various factors, including genetic predispositions, environmental influences, and lifestyle choices. Physical diseases can manifest as a wide spectrum of disorders, ranging from infectious illnesses caused by microorganisms to chronic conditions like cardiovascular diseases, autoimmune disorders, and cancers.

The hallmark of a physical disease is its impact on the body's physiological processes, disrupting the delicate balance required for optimal health. Diagnosis and treatment often involve a combination of medical interventions, lifestyle modifications, and preventive measures to restore or manage the body's equilibrium and mitigate the impact of the disease on overall well-being.

Mental and Psychological Diseases in The Seventh Realm

Mental and psychological diseases encompass a broad spectrum of conditions that affect cognition, emotions, behavior, and overall mental well-being. These disorders range from mood disorders like depression and bipolar disorder to anxiety disorders, schizophrenia, and various forms of neurodevelopmental disorders.

Unlike physical diseases, mental and psychological ailments often involve disturbances in thought processes, emotions, and social functioning. These conditions can result from a combination of genetic, biological, environmental, and psychological factors. The manifestations of mental and psychological diseases can be diverse, impacting a person's ability to cope with the demands of daily life, maintain relationships, and experience a satisfactory quality of life.

Diagnosis and treatment typically involve a combination of psychotherapy, medication, and support services, emphasizing the importance of a holistic approach to address both the biological and psychosocial aspects of disease.

Contemplating the Biblical and Spiritual Concepts of Internal, External, and Mental Diseases

Spiritual Disease in The Seventh Realm

Spiritual disease refers to a condition affecting the innermost essence of an individual, impacting their spiritual well-being, values, and connection to a higher power or inner self.

Unlike physical ailments, spiritual diseases are not tangible or easily quantifiable; instead, they manifest as disruptions in one's sense of purpose, inner peace, or ethical compass.

These afflictions may arise from various sources, such as moral conflicts, existential crises, or a sense of disconnection from one's spiritual beliefs.

Spiritual diseases can manifest in the form of despair, apathy, or a lack of meaning in life.

Healing from spiritual disease often involves introspection, self-discovery, and a journey towards aligning one's actions and beliefs with a deeper sense of purpose or higher power and fostering a sense of balance and fulfillment at the spiritual level.

Research suggests that individuals with a strong spiritual foundation tend to exhibit lower levels of stress, which is a known contributor to various physical ailments.

The power of positive beliefs and a sense of meaning in life can contribute to resilience, enabling individuals to cope more effectively with the challenges that may otherwise exacerbate physical health issues.

The practice of mindfulness, meditation, and prayer, often integral to spiritual wellness, has been associated with improved physical and physiological wellness. Specific clinical entities studied included improved symptom control of mental disorders, reduced physiologic symptoms, such as pain, improved immune function, and better cardiovascular health.

Contemplating the Biblical and Spiritual Concepts of Internal, External, and Mental Diseases

Spiritual Consciousness and Spiritual Wellness Affects Physical Disease

The complex relationship between spiritual consciousness and physical health is a subject that transcends the boundaries of conventional medicine and delves into the realm of holistic well-being. Spiritual consciousness, often rooted in a sense of purpose, connection to a higher power, or inner self-awareness, can significantly influence the development and progression of physical diseases.

Moreover, spiritual consciousness can motivate individuals to adopt healthier lifestyles, such as engaging in regular physical activity, maintaining a balanced diet, and avoiding harmful habits, thereby reducing the risk of chronic diseases.

While the connection between spiritual consciousness and physical health is complex, it underscores the importance of addressing the holistic well-being of individuals, recognizing that spiritual wellness can play a pivotal role in promoting and sustaining physical well-being.

Spiritual Consciousness and Spiritual Wellness Affects Mental and Psychological Diseases

The relationship between spiritual consciousness and mental well-being is extremely complex and can significantly influence mental and psychological health. Spiritual wellness, rooted in a deep connection to one's purpose, values, or a higher power, holds the potential to influence the development and management of mental and psychological diseases.

Individuals with a strong spiritual foundation often report enhanced emotional resilience and coping mechanisms, protecting against the stresses that can contribute to conditions like anxiety and depression.

Practices such as meditation, prayer, or contemplation, central to spiritual consciousness, have demonstrated benefits in reducing symptoms of various mental health disorders. Furthermore, a sense of spiritual meaning and purpose in life can act as a protective factor, offering individuals a framework to navigate challenges and find solace in times of emotional distress.

The fostering of positive beliefs and a spiritual support system can contribute to a more optimistic outlook, aiding in the prevention and recovery from mental health issues. While the relationship between spiritual wellness and mental health is complicated, it underscores the importance of recognizing and integrating the spiritual dimension in mental health care, acknowledging its potential as a valuable resource for fostering emotional well-being and resilience.

The Exercise- The Mindfulness and Meditation Practice for The Seventh Realm

The Mindfulness and Meditation Practice for The Seventh Realm

The healing miracles performed by Jesus, as recorded in the New Testament of the Bible, are symbolic representations of spiritual and physical restoration. (Spend at least 5 mins contemplating each section.)

Consider the Woman with the Issue of Blood (Mark 5:25-34, Matthew 9:20-22, Luke 8:43-48):

- Description: A woman suffering from a chronic issue of bleeding for twelve years touches the hem of Jesus's garment and is instantly healed.
- Symbolism: This miracle highlights the power of faith and the accessibility of healing through a simple touch. It emphasizes the inclusivity of Jesus's healing ministry and the transformative nature of faith.

In 'The7Realms', the woman with an issue of blood symbolizes the higher spiritual consciousness concepts of *Seeking and Knocking*- believing and manifesting. In this case, manifesting healing. Imagine the faith and courage it must have taken for this woman to push her way through the crowd to touch Jesus' garment and believe that she would be healed.

Consider the Healing of Leprosy (Matthew 8:1-4, Mark 1:40-45, Luke 5:12-16):

- Description: Jesus heals a man afflicted with leprosy, a highly stigmatized and contagious skin disease.
- Symbolism: Leprosy was not only a physical ailment but also carried social and religious stigma. Jesus's healing reflects the restoration of both physical health and social acceptance. It underscores Jesus's authority over impurity and his willingness to touch and heal the marginalized.

Each miracle carries its own significance, addressing different aspects of human suffering and illustrating the breadth of Jesus's compassion and divine power. These miracles can also symbolize the power Higher Spiritual Consciousness outlined in **The First Realm- The Trinity- God the Son** in 'The7Realms'.

The Mindfulness and Meditation Practice for The Seventh Realm

In essence, each healing miracle of Jesus goes beyond the physical cure, pointing to deeper spiritual truths. (Spend at least 5 mins contemplating each section.)

Consider the Healing of the Blind (Matthew 9:27-31, Matthew 20:29-34, Mark 8:22-26, John 9:1-12):

- Description: Jesus restores sight to blind individuals in various instances.
- Symbolism: Blindness often symbolizes spiritual blindness in the Gospels. Jesus's healing of the blind not only addresses physical infirmity but also signifies the illumination of spiritual understanding. It emphasizes the transformative power of encountering Jesus.

Consider the Demon-Possessed (Mark 5:1-20, Matthew 8:28-34, Luke 8:26-39):

- Description: Jesus exorcises demons from a man living among the tombs.
- Symbolism: This miracle illustrates Jesus's authority over spiritual forces and his role as the liberator from demonic oppression. It emphasizes the transformative power of encountering Jesus, leading to the restoration of mental and emotional well-being.

In The Seventh Realm, the healings of Jesus Christ represent the restoration of faith, social inclusion, spiritual insight, and freedom from spiritual bondage, demonstrating Jesus's compassion and his transformative impact on individuals' lives.

The Mindfulness and Meditation Practice for The Seventh Realm

In **The Seventh Realm**, you are asked to consider that the healing miracles attributed to Jesus in the New Testament serve as powerful narratives that extend beyond mere demonstrations of supernatural abilities. (Spend at least 2-3 mins contemplating each bullet point.)

1. In The Seventh Realm, consider the Symbolic Representations of Spiritual Restoration:

- **Faith and Salvation**: Many of Jesus's healing miracles emphasize the importance of faith. The woman with the issue of blood, for instance, is healed because of her unwavering faith in Jesus's ability to bring about healing. This underscores the spiritual principle that faith plays a crucial role in the process of salvation and restoration.

- **Cleansing from Sin**: Miracles such as the healing of leprosy carry a symbolic weight. Leprosy, in addition to being a physical ailment, was considered a metaphor for sin and impurity in the cultural context. Jesus's healing not only restores physical health but also symbolizes the cleansing of the soul from sin, emphasizing the transformative power of spiritual redemption.

- **Illumination and Spiritual Understanding**: Healing the blind serves as a metaphor for the enlightenment of the spiritual senses. Jesus's ability to restore sight symbolizes the opening of spiritual eyes, allowing individuals to perceive and understand the truths of God. It underscores the idea that encountering Jesus brings about a profound change in one's spiritual perception.

2. In The Seventh Realm, consider the Symbolic Representations of Physical Restoration:

- **Social Inclusion**: Miracles like the healing of leprosy also address the societal implications of illness. Leprosy carried not only physical suffering but also social isolation. Jesus's healing emphasizes the restoration of not just physical health but also social acceptance, challenging cultural norms and prejudices.

- **Freedom from Oppression**: The healing of the demon-possessed illustrates Jesus's authority over spiritual forces. Beyond the physical symptoms, this miracle symbolizes liberation from spiritual bondage and oppression. It communicates the idea that encountering Jesus leads to freedom from the forces that hold individual's captive.

The Mindfulness and Meditation Practice for The Seventh Realm

The healing miracles are rich in symbolism, conveying profound messages about spiritual and physical restoration, the nature of human suffering, and the compassionate power of Jesus. (Spend at least 2-3 mins contemplating each bullet point.)

3. The Seventh Realm illustrates the Breadth of Jesus's Compassion and Divine Power:

- **Compassion for the Marginalized**: Jesus's choice to heal those considered outcasts or socially marginalized, such as the woman with the issue of blood or the demon-possessed man, underscores his compassion for the downtrodden. These miracles challenge societal norms and demonstrate the inclusive nature of Jesus's love and healing power.

- **Demonstration of Divine Authority**: Each healing miracle serves as a demonstration of Jesus's divine authority over both the physical and spiritual realms. Whether calming storms, raising the dead, or healing diseases, these miracles emphasize Jesus's role as the divine source of restoration and redemption.

In conclusion, **The Seventh Realm** considers the healing miracles in the New Testament as symbolic narratives that go beyond the physical act of healing. They are symbolic representations of spiritual truths, conveying messages about faith, salvation, cleansing from sin, societal inclusion, freedom from oppression, and the compassionate power of Jesus. These stories collectively illustrate the breadth and depth of Jesus's transformative impact on both the spiritual and physical dimensions of human existence.

Questions for Week 10/Lesson 10
[Remember to practice **The Mindfulness and Meditation Exercise** associated with this lesson *after completing each daily question*.]

Week 10: Day 1

Contemplate the concept of **'Disease Manifestation- Internal, External, and Psychological Diseases'** (the lowest realm of Lower Spiritual Consciousness- Spiritual Unwellness). How is related to **the spiritual entropy**? [Remember, The Seventh Realm progresses from The Fifth Realm of 'Condemnation, Fear, and Worry' and The Sixth Realm of 'Unforgiveness, Anger, and Doubt'.]

_____
_____
_____
_____
_____
_____
_____
_____
_____
_____
_____
_____
_____
_____
_____

Week 10: Day 2

Contemplate the meaning/concept of **Internal Diseases**. What are some biblical examples of Internal Diseases?

Week 10: Day 3

Contemplate the meaning/concept of **External Diseases**. What are some biblical examples of External Diseases?

Week 10: Day 4

Contemplate the meaning/concept of **Mental/Psychological Diseases**. What are some biblical examples of Mental/Psychological Diseases?

Week 10: Day 5

Based on the biblical examples of Jesus' healing Internal Diseases, what might the healing of Internal Diseases represent from a spiritual perspective?

Week 10: Day 6

Based on the biblical examples of Jesus' healing External Diseases, what might the healing of External Diseases represent from a spiritual perspective?

Week 10: Day 7

Based on the biblical examples of Jesus' healing Mental/Psychological Diseases, what might the healing of Mental/Psychological Diseases represent from a spiritual perspective?

_____
_____
_____
_____
_____
_____
_____
_____
_____
_____
_____
_____
_____
_____
_____
_____
_____

Week 11/ Lesson 11: The Anchoring, Opening and Transitioning Mantras of 'The7Realms'- The Inner Hum, The Amen, and The Breath

Lesson 11: The Anchoring, Opening and Transitioning Mantras of 'The7Realms'-

The Inner Hum, The Amen, & The Breath

11.1- Anchoring- The Inner Hum

11.2- The Opening Mantra- The Amen

11.3- Transitioning- The Breath

Questions for Week 11/Lesson 11

11.1- Anchoring- The Inner Hum

Anchoring - The Inner Hum

What is Anchoring?

Anchoring in mindfulness and meditation refers to the practice of using a specific focus point to stabilize the mind and bring one's attention to the present moment.

This technique is central to mindfulness practices and can be particularly useful for beginners or anyone struggling with scattered thoughts or restlessness.

The anchor can be anything that can be consistently returned to whenever the mind wanders. Common anchors breathing (or the breath), sounds, visual objects, and phrases or mantras.

The purpose of anchoring is not to prevent the mind from wandering but to provide a gentle means of returning to the present moment when it does.

It helps cultivate a state of awareness and acceptance of the present experience, reducing the tendency to get caught up in thoughts about the past or worries about the future. Over time, this practice can lead to increased calm, clarity, and insight.

Finding Your Inner Vibrational Hum

One of the principle anchoring and centering methods of 'The7Realms' Mindfulness and Meditation practices involves "humming". The purpose of humming in 'The7Realms' is employed as a technique to quiet the mind and allow you to focus your spiritual energy.

This focus of spiritual energy is usually directed at the realm of spiritual consciousness you wish to attain during meditation.

Humming is often used in different cultures as an initial opening and a final closing in a particular meditation practice. *The Hum* (as it is called in 'The7Realms') is used in very much the same way in 'The7Realms'.

Anchoring- The Inner Hum

The Meaning of Hum, To Hum, or Humming

The term "hum" can have various meanings depending on the context in which it is used. Here are a few different definitions:

1. As a noun, "hum" can refer to a low, continuous sound, often produced by machinery, engines, or other vibrating sources.

2. As a verb, "hum" can mean to make a low, continuous sound or to produce a steady, murmuring noise. People may *hum* a tune, and bees can *hum* as they fly.

3. In a metaphorical sense, "hum" can describe a state of busyness or activity, as in "the city was alive and vibrant with the *hum* of life."

4. In certain contexts, "hum" can also refer to a sound made by people when they are thinking or pondering something. For example, someone might *hum* in thought while trying to remember something.

The precise meaning of "hum" in each context can vary, so it's important to consider the specific usage and surrounding context to understand its intended meaning.

The Spiritual Significance of "Humming"

In some spiritual and meditative practices, humming or chanting specific sounds or mantras is used as a way to focus the mind, create a calming atmosphere, and induce a meditative state. For example:

1. In Hinduism, there's a practice known as "Om" or "Aum" chanting, where the sacred sound "Om" is repeated to aid in meditation and connect with the divine.

2. Buddhist monks may engage in chanting, including the repetition of sutras or mantras, to achieve a state of mindfulness and enlightenment.

3. Some New Age and holistic wellness practices incorporate humming as a form of vibrational healing or energy work.

4. In Sufi Islamic traditions, there are practices of chanting and remembrance, often accompanied by repetitive vocal sounds, to attain spiritual connection and inner peace.

The specific spiritual significance and practices associated with humming can vary greatly among different cultures and belief systems. It's important to consider the context and tradition in which humming is being used to understand its spiritual implications.

Anchoring- The Inner Hum

Humming in 'The7Realms' Mindfulness and Meditation

The humming technique in 'The7Realms' Mindfulness and Meditation practice is used to enhance focus, relaxation, and the overall meditative experience. The humming technique used in 'The7Realms' involves producing specific vocal sounds or vibrations, which can have several unique benefits:

1. **Centering and Grounding**: Humming specific sounds can help you ground yourself in the present moment. The act of producing these vibrations can provide for you a physical anchor for meditation, making it easier to stay focused and centered.

2. **Calming the Mind**: The gentle, continuous sound of humming can have a soothing effect on the mind. It can reduce your mental chatter and distractions, making it easier for you to enter a state of calm and relaxation.

3. **Vibrational Healing**: Some believe that specific sound frequencies and vibrations can have a healing effect on your body and mind. By humming certain sounds, you can promote balance and harmony within your mind, body, and soul.

4. **Chakra Balancing**: In practices such as yoga and certain forms of meditation, humming may be used to balance and align the body's energy centers, known as chakras. Different vocal sounds are associated with specific chakras, and by producing these sounds, practitioners aim to balance their energy flow.

5. **Enhanced Breath Awareness**: Humming often involve you controlling your breath and producing sounds with intention. This can deepen your awareness of the breath and encourage conscious, rhythmic breathing, which is a fundamental aspect of many meditation techniques.

Anchoring- The Inner Hum

The Use of Humming in 'The7Realms' Mindfulness and Meditation Practice is as follows:

1. Find a Quiet Space: Choose a quiet and comfortable place where you can meditate without interruptions.

2. Sit Comfortably: Sit in a comfortable position with your back straight. You can also practice these techniques while lying down if that is more comfortable for you.

3. Close Your Eyes: Close your eyes to minimize external distractions.

4. Focus on Your Breath: Begin by focusing on your natural breath for a few moments to settle into the meditation.

5. Start Humming: In 'The7Realms' we begin with a low, under-the-breath but purposeful sound... *Humm..., Humm.... Humm...* You can choose a sound or mantra that resonates with you. You can use traditional sounds like "Om" or any sound that feels soothing and calming to you. Start producing the sound gently and continuously.

6. Concentrate on the Vibration: Pay close attention to the physical sensation of the sound as you produce it. Feel the vibrations in your body.

7. Maintain Your Focus: Continue humming for the duration of your meditation session. If your mind wanders, gently bring your focus back to the sound and the vibrations.

8. Conclude Mindfully: When you're ready to transition to the next phase of 'The7Realms' meditation, gradually reduce the sound until it fades away. Sit quietly for a few moments before opening your eyes and resuming the next step.

9. This technique is used in the opening and closing of the formal Mindfulness and Meditation Practices of 'The7Realms'.

It's important to remember that the effectiveness of humming in meditation and mindfulness practices can vary from person to person. Experiment with different sounds and techniques to find what works best for you and enhances your meditative experience.

11.2- The Opening Mantra- The Amen

The Opening Mantra- The Amen

What is a Mantra?

In mindfulness and meditation, a mantra is a word, sound, or phrase repeated to aid concentration and foster a deep state of meditation or mindfulness. In 'The7Realms', the word 'Amen' is used as both an opening and a centering mantra during both mindfulness and meditation practices. Mantras serve several purposes:

1. **Focus**: They help the mind focus by providing a constant point of attention, which can be especially helpful for beginners or those with a busy mind.

2. **Peacefulness and Calming**: The repetition of a mantra can induce a state of deep relaxation and mental tranquillity, as the rhythmic nature of the repetition can be soothing.

3. **Intention and Attention:** Mantras often carry meanings or intentions that can influence the meditator's state of mind, promoting qualities like peace, compassion, or strength.

4. **Vibrational Energy**: Some traditions believe in the vibrational power of sounds, where the sound of the mantra itself is said to have beneficial effects on the body and mind.

Different cultures and different spiritual practices use different mantras. In mindfulness practice, mantras can also be simple, secular phrases or words that don't necessarily have a religious connotation but are used to support the practice of presence and awareness. The effectiveness of a mantra is not just in its meaning or sound, but in its consistent use as a tool to return the mind to the present and reduce distractions.

Mindfulness and Meditation

- Daily Mindfulness: Beyond formal meditation sessions, you can use 'Amen' in your daily life as a reminder to stay mindful and present. For instance, when you find yourself lost in thought or rushing through a task, you can quietly say 'Amen' to bring your attention back to the current moment.

- Meditation and Universal Connection: In 'The7Realms' meditation session, 'Amen' can also represent an acknowledgment of the interconnectedness of all living beings and a shared human experience. It can serve as a reminder that, despite individual differences, there are universal truths and experiences that bind us together.

The Opening Mantra- The Amen

Understanding the Meaning and Definitions of 'Amen'

"Amen" is a word that holds various meanings and significance across different contexts, including its literal, universal, spiritual, and Christian definitions:

1. **Literal Definition**: Literally, the word 'Amen' is an ancient Semitic word that means 'I believe', "so be it" or "truly." It is often used at the end of a prayer or statement to express agreement, affirmation, or a desire for the words to be fulfilled.

2. **Universal Definition**: 'Amen' is a term used in various religious and spiritual traditions around the world, not just within Christianity. It is often employed to signify the conclusion of a prayer or a statement of belief, essentially expressing the hope or certainty that what has been said is true and will come to pass.

3. **Spiritual Definition**: In a broader spiritual context, 'Amen' represents a form of acknowledgment and alignment with divine will or universal truths. It can be seen as an affirmation of one's faith and trust in a higher power, the universe, or spiritual principles.

4. **Christian Definition**: In Christianity, 'Amen' holds particular significance. It is used extensively in Christian worship, prayer, and scripture. In this context, "Amen" is often used to conclude prayers and hymns, indicating the congregation's agreement with the words spoken and a submission to God's will. It serves as a solemn affirmation of faith and the acceptance of God's authority.

In Christian theology, Jesus is often referred to as the 'Amen' in the New Testament. This is based on passages like Revelation 3:14 (ESV), which states: "And to the angel of the church in Laodicea write: 'The words of the Amen, the faithful and true witness, the beginning of God's creation.'"

In 'The7Realms', 'Amen' is a word used to indicate agreement, affirmation, and alignment with spiritual or divine truths. While it is widely recognized as a Christian term, it is not exclusive to Christianity and has a universal and spiritual significance that extends beyond any one religious' tradition.

The Opening Mantra- The Amen

The Use of 'Amen' in Mindfulness and Meditation

In 'The7Realms' Mindfulness and Meditation practices, 'Amen' can be used as a powerful tool to deepen your connection to the present moment and enhance the overall experience.

- **Affirmation of Presence**: When used in the opening of 'The7Realms' meditation session, 'Amen' serves as an affirmation of presence. It signifies a conscious decision to be fully engaged in the present moment, setting a clear intention for the meditation practice. By saying 'Amen', you're affirming your commitment to the here and now, leaving behind distractions and mental clutter.

- **Focusing the Mind**: During meditation, the mind can often wander or become entangled in thoughts and worries. Incorporating "Amen" at moments of distraction can act as a gentle reminder to refocus your attention on the meditation object, whether it's the breath, a mantra, or a specific sensation. It's like saying, "Let go of the distractions, return to this moment."

- **Affirming Gratitude**: 'Amen' can also be used to express gratitude for the present moment. This reinforces positive emotions and a sense of contentment.

- **Release of Tension**: In moments of tension, stress, or discomfort during meditation, "Amen" can be used as a release valve. By vocalizing 'Amen', you can let go of tension, emotional baggage, and resistance, allowing yourself to relax more deeply into the meditation practice.

- **Alignment with Intention**: In 'The7Realms' meditation session, if you have set an intention, such as cultivating compassion, patience, or inner peace, 'Amen' can be used to reaffirm that intention. It's a way of reinforcing your commitment to the purpose of the practice.

- **Conclusion and Closure**: At the end of 'The7Realms' meditation session, 'Amen' can be used to conclude the practice. It signals the end of the session and encapsulates the experience. It's a way of recognizing that the meditation has come to its natural conclusion and that you're ready to transition back into your daily life.

Overall, the use of 'Amen' in 'The7Realms' and in secular mindfulness and meditation practices offers a versatile and meaningful way to anchor oneself in the present moment, affirm intentions, and deepen the connection with the here and now. It can be adapted to individual preferences and can significantly enhance the mindfulness experience.

11.3- Transitioning- The Breath

Transitioning- The Breath

Breath and Spirit

In 'The7Realms', the *breath* is used as a mantra for transitioning between focused prayer and scriptural meditations. The specific breath mantras used in 'The7Realms' are: *'The Breath of God'; 'The Breath of Spirit'; and 'The Breath of Life'*. In the practice of 'The7Realms', breath is frequently employed as a means to connect with the divine, to align oneself with the patterns of the universe, and to deepen one's awareness of being part of a larger whole.

Breath is often seen as the counterpart to the concept of Spirit. In many cultures and spiritual traditions, the word for "breath" is synonymous with life force or spirit. For example, in Sanskrit, "prana", in Hebrew, "ruach", and in Greek, "pneuma", all broadly translate to breath, life, spirit, or soul. This linguistic relationship suggests a thoughtful recognition of breath as more than a mere physical process. It is also viewed as the essence of life.

From a metaphysical standpoint, **breath is considered the bridge between the mind, body, and soul, connecting our physical existence with our higher consciousness.**

In moments of deep breathing, one might feel a sense of expansion beyond the physical self, touching upon a more profound sense of peace, presence, and connection. This experience is at the heart of many spiritual practices and meditations, which use breath as a vehicle to transcend the physical limitations of the body and reach a heightened state of spiritual awareness. Through mindful breathing, individuals are not just filling their bodies with oxygen; they are also nourishing their spirits, fostering a sense of harmony, balance, and unity.

Additionally, breath is inherently linked to the cycles of nature and the universe, echoing the ebb and flow of life itself. This universal rhythm of breath is a constant reminder of the interconnectedness of all things, fostering a sense of oneness and compassion.

By consciously engaging with our breath, we align ourselves with the vibration and spiritual energy of the universe, tapping into a reservoir of peace and wisdom that transcends the individual. In this way, breath serves not only as a sustenance of life but as a spiritual connector to the Consciousness, guiding us toward a deeper understanding of ourselves and the universe.

Transitioning- The Breath

Breathing in Mindfulness and Meditation

In 'The7Realms', breath serves as the cornerstone of mindfulness and meditation practices, acting as a conscious and subconscious force that bridges the transition between the mind, body, and soul. It is a natural act of the body with a natural rhythm. An intimate act of life that is uniquely both involuntary and voluntary.

In the mindfulness practice of 'The7Realms', breath acts as an anchor, for you to return to when the mind wanders. This simple, repetitive **focus on the breath helps to cultivate a state of present moment awareness**, training the mind to dwell in the current experience without judgment. It teaches patience and acceptance of the present moment.

In the meditation practice of 'The7Realms', the act of deep, mindful breathing is known to induce a relaxation response, countering the stress and anxiety that plague our daily lives. By consciously regulating our breath- slowing it down, deepening it- we send signals to the brain to calm the nervous system.

This shift from a state of over-stimulation to one of relaxation is fundamental in meditation practices, paving the way for deeper states of peace and insight. **Through breath, we learn to temper our emotional responses, gain clarity, and enhance our overall mental and physical well-being.** Furthermore, breath is universally accessible and constantly available, making it an open tool in the practice of mindfulness.

It requires no special equipment, environment, or even physical ability, and can be practiced by anyone, anywhere. This universality makes breath an ideal focal point for mindfulness and meditation, providing a common way for individuals to explore inner tranquillity and wisdom.

As we deepen our relationship with our breath, we deepen our connection to ourselves and the world around us, fostering a sense of interconnectedness and compassion that is the heart of a mindfulness and meditation practice.

Transitioning- The Breath

The Breath- Intermediary Mantras in 'The7Realms'

'The7Realms' uses three intermediary mantras in between meditation scriptures. These intermediary mantras are- "The breath of God", 'The breath of Spirit', and "The breath of Life".

The Breath of God

The 'breath of God' is a symbolic term found in numerous religious texts and traditions, primarily within Christianity and Judaism, that signifies the life-giving power, presence, and spirit of God. This concept highlights the belief that God's breath is a source of life, creation, and spiritual vitality. It is often used to describe the divine force that animates and sustains all living beings and the universe itself. In 2 Timothy 3:16, the Bible states that "All Scripture is God-breathed and is useful for teaching, correcting and training in righteousness," indicating that the Scriptures are inspired by God's spirit. Thus, the "breath of God" is a profound symbol of God's life-giving essence, divine inspiration, spiritual presence, and transformative power within mindfulness and meditative practices.

The Breath of Spirit

The term 'breath of Spirit' encompasses the idea of a life-giving, energizing, or purifying force attributed to a divine or spiritual source. It's closely related to the concept of the "breath of God" in religious traditions, particularly within the context of the Holy Spirit in Christianity. In Christianity, the Holy Spirit is considered the third person of the Trinity, embodying God's presence in the world. The "breath of Spirit" in this context refers to the presence, guidance, and comfort the Holy Spirit provides to believers. It is the Holy Spirit who empowers, guides, and sanctifies individuals, drawing them closer to God. In some interpretations, the "breath of Spirit" is seen as a unifying force that connects all believers, transcending individual differences to create a sense of community and shared faith.

The Breath of Life

The phrase 'breath of life' has its roots in many religious, spiritual, and philosophical traditions, where it commonly refers to the vital force that animates living beings. This concept is deeply embedded in the idea that life itself is a gift from a divine or supernatural source, represented by the act of breathing or the presence of breath. In the Judeo-Christian tradition, the "breath of life" is first mentioned in the book of Genesis in the Bible. Genesis 2:7 states, "Then the Lord God formed a man from the dust of the ground and breathed into his nostrils the breath of life, and the man became a living being." It underscores the belief that life itself is a divine gift and that the spirit or soul is what fundamentally distinguishes living beings from inanimate matter.

The Gift of 'The7Realms'

Questions for Week 11/Lesson 11

Week 11: Day 1

What is meant by the term **anchoring** in Mindfulness and Meditation?

Week 11: Day 2

How is **humming** used as an anchoring method in Mindfulness and Meditation practices?

_____
_____
_____
_____
_____
_____
_____
_____
_____
_____
_____
_____
_____
_____
_____
_____
_____

Week 11: Day 3

What is meant by the term **mantra** in Mindfulness and Meditation?

Week 11: Day 4

What are the different meanings and definitions of the word **Amen**? What is the importance of **Amen** from the Christian perspective?

Week 11: Day 5

How is the word **Amen** used in Mindfulness and Meditation practices?

Week 11: Day 6

Why is the concept of **'Breath' or 'Breathing'** important in Mindfulness and Meditation? How does the word **'Breath'** relate to Spirit?

_____
_____
_____
_____
_____
_____
_____
_____
_____
_____
_____
_____
_____
_____
_____
_____
_____

Week 11: Day 7

How is the practice of **'Breath'** used in the Mindfulness and Meditation practice of 'The7Realms'? What are the 3 intermediary mantras of breath in 'The7Realms'?

Week 12/ Lesson 12: Conclusion- The Step-by-Step Explanation of The Meditation Process - 'The7Realms' Meditation

Lesson 12: Conclusion The Step-by-Step Explanation of The Meditation Process – 'The7Realms' Meditation

12.1- The Practice of 'The7Realms' in Mindfulness and Meditation

12.2- The Structure and Organization of The Seven Realms of Spiritual Consciousness: The Pyramid of Sovereignty

12.3- An Overview of How to Use 'The7Realms' Mindfulness and Meditation Practice

12.4- Examples of Anchoring Prayer(s)

12.5- Comprehensive Practice of 'The7Realms'- STEP 1

12.6- Comprehensive Practice of 'The7Realms'- STEP 2

12.7- Comprehensive Practice of 'The7Realms'- STEP 3- Final Step

Questions for Week 12/Lesson 12

12.1- The Practice of 'The7Realms' in Mindfulness and Meditation

'The7Realms' Mindfulness and Meditation Practice

The Seven Trilateral Realms of Spiritual Consciousness- *A Newly Defined Christian Pathway to Higher Consciousness through Biblical Meditation* (aka 'The7Realms'), is a transformational work that uncovers 84 biblical words and scriptures across revealing a hidden pathway to higher consciousness. The ordering and organization of these words and scriptures was given to me as a divine spiritual gift.

This pathway allows us to transcend from our usual states of subconscious thinking (lower spiritual consciousness) to an enhanced state of spiritual enlightenment and spiritual awakening (higher spiritual consciousness). We can accomplish this by using the newly discovered trilateral words and scriptures from the Bible.

'The7Realms' invites you to travel along this new path to higher spiritual consciousness *(Christian Mindfulness),* by way of focused prayer on these specifically outlined words and scriptures *(Biblical Meditation)*. Each of these realms is made up of a trilateral concept (three inter-related biblical words). Each realm exists within and corresponds to a given level of spiritual consciousness. Each of these biblical words is matched with specific trilateral biblical scriptures.

Christian Mindfulness is the act of centering our awareness or focus on the Word of God in the form of focused prayer (attention).

The trilateral words act as a guidepost or anchoring words, or mantras, to let us know, or remind us, where we exist, at any given moment, in spiritual consciousness, and in which specific realm our thoughts reside.

Based on the discovery of 'The7Realms', this scriptural meditation (intention) represents Biblical Meditation. This Biblical Meditation is based on specific trilateral words and scriptures that represent a distinct realm of spiritual consciousness.

This practice is meant hopefully to lead to a destination of higher spiritual awareness and enlightenment.

12.2- The Structure and Organization of The Seven Realms of Spiritual Consciousness: The Pyramid of Sovereignty

Ryan C. Neal, MD

The Structure and Organization of The Seven Realms of Spiritual Consciousness

The Pyramid of Sovereignty

-The Primary Pyramid

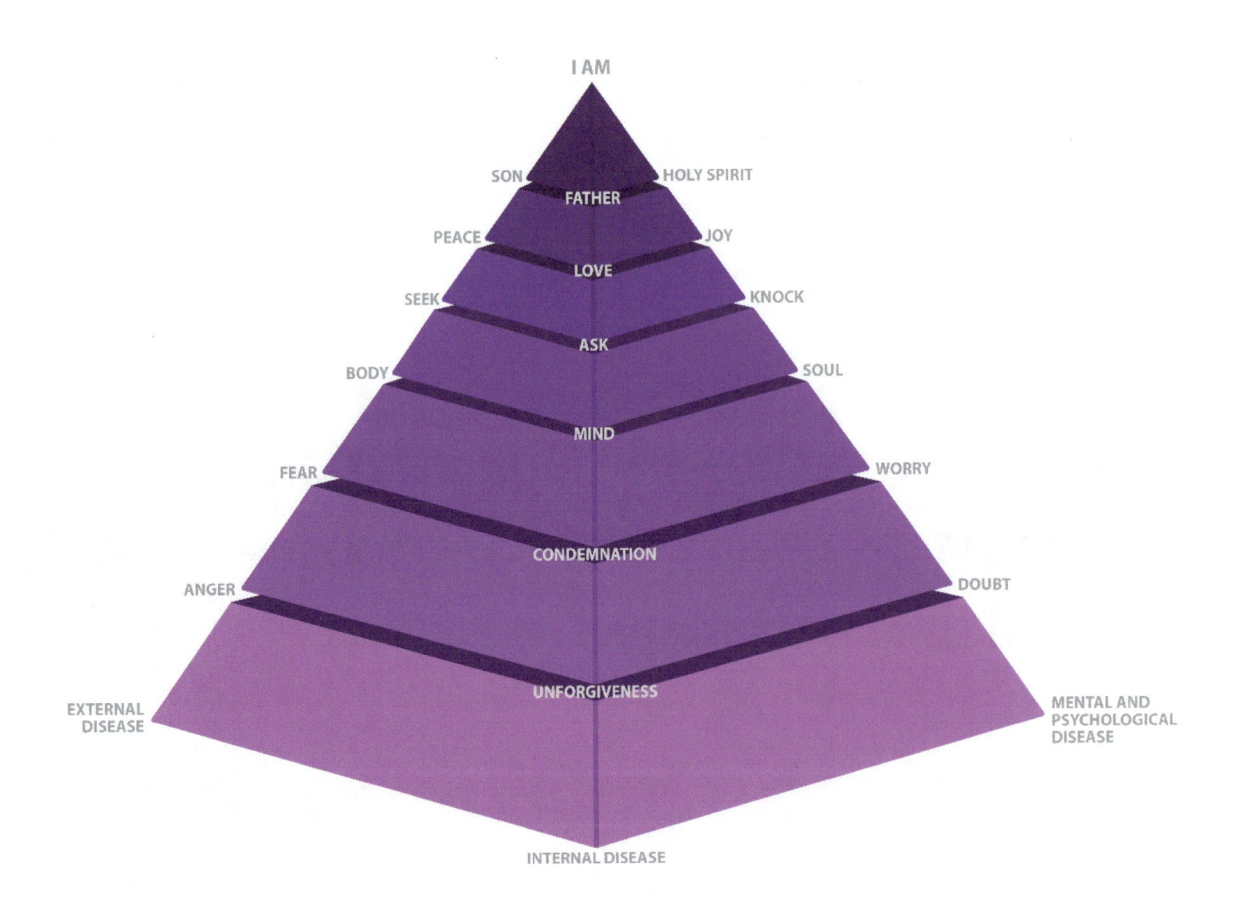

(Illustration 2- The Pyramid of Sovereignty)

The Structure and Organization of The Seven Realms of Spiritual Consciousness

The Seven Trilateral Realms of **The Pyramid of Sovereignty**:

The First Trilateral Realm of Spiritual Consciousness

- The Realm of The Trinity- God the Father, God the Son, and God the Holy Spirit

The Second Trilateral Realm of Spiritual Consciousness

- The Realm of Love, Peace, and Joy- The Realm of "Fruit of The Spirit"

The Third Trilateral Realm of Spiritual Consciousness

- The Realm of Ask, Seek and Knock-The Realms of Manifestation

The Fourth Trilateral Realm of Spiritual Consciousness

- The Realm of Mind, Body, and Soul (MBS)- The Mental, The Physical and The Spiritual

The Fifth Trilateral Realm of Spiritual Consciousness

- The Realm of Self-Condemnation, Fear and Worry

The Sixth Trilateral Realm of Spiritual Consciousness

- The Realm of Unforgiveness (Hatred), Anger and Doubt

The Seventh Trilateral Realm of Spiritual Consciousness

- The Realm of Internal Disease, External Disease, and Mental and Psychological Disease- The Realm of Disease Manifestation

12.3- An Overview of How to Use 'The7Realms' Mindfulness and Meditation Practice

The Mindfulness and Meditation Practice - Overview of The Seven Realms

The Seven Trilateral Realms of Spiritual Consciousness (Spiritual Wellness)	The Seven Realms- Highest to Lowest
The Realm of The Trinity - God the Father - God the Son - God the Holy Spirit	The First Realm Highest Realm of Spiritual Consciousness and Spiritual Wellness The Realm of Physical Wellness
The Realm of the Fruit of The Spirit - Love - Peace - Joy	The Second Realm The Realm of Co-existence in The Spirit
The Realm of Manifestation - Ask - Seek - Knock	The Third Realm The Realm of Manifestation from Spiritual Consciousness
The Realm of Consciousness - Mind - Body - Soul	The Fourth Realm The Realm of Spiritual Transition from Lower to Higher Consciousness
The Realm of Condemnation - Condemnation - Fear - Worry	The Fifth Realm The Initial Realm of Transition into Spiritual Entropy *(The First Realm of Lower Consciousness)*
The Realm of Hatred (Self-hatred) - Unforgiveness - Anger - Doubt	The Sixth Realm The Carnal Descent into Lower Consciousness Thoughts, Feeling, and Emotions *(The precursor of physical disease)*
The Realm of Disease Manifestation - Internal Disease - External Disease - Mental/Psychological Disease	The Seventh Realm The Lowest Realm of Spiritual Consciousness and Spiritual Unwellness *(The Realm of Physical Disease)*

The Mindfulness and Meditation Practice- Overview of The Seven Realms

An Overview of How to Use 'The7Realms' Mindfulness and Meditation Practice- STEP 1:

STEP 1: Identify the Realm of Spiritual Consciousness You Exist in Now and Start the Meditation Process Here.

Phase 1: Identify your Thoughts, Feelings, and/or Emotions (TFEs).

Suppose you realize that your Thoughts, Feelings, and/or Emotions (TFEs) are centered around *being anxious, worried, or fearful*. Maybe you are anxious about something that is happening in your life, on your job, or in your relationship.

Anxiety is related to the word **fear**. Fear is one of the most common negative emotions anyone can experience. The word fear appears in the Bible over 365 times. (That's a 'fear' for every day of the year.)

Phase 2: Identify which Realm of Spiritual Consciousness your TFE exists within

In 'The7Realms', anxiety can be found in **The 5th Realm of Spiritual Consciousness- The Realm of Condemnation, Fear, and Worry.**

Once you recognize that you're in this realm, you are now aware that you exist in a state of Lower Spiritual Consciousness (LSC).

This state often exists in the subconscious where much of your spiritual unwellness resides.

Phase 3: Choose the practice of Mindfulness or Meditation

Once you identify that you are in a Lower Spiritual Consciousness Realm (The 5th Realm), you would choose a path of Mindfulness or Meditation to transcend to Higher Spiritual Consciousness. You would then choose a *trilateral word* (for the Mindfulness practice) or a *trilateral scripture* (for the Meditation practice).

The Mindfulness and Meditation Practice- Overview of The Seven Realms

An Overview of How to Use 'The7Realms' Mindfulness and Meditation Practice- STEP 1:

STEP 1 (cont.): Identify the Realm of Spiritual Consciousness You Exist in Now and Start the Meditation Process Here.

Phase 3a: Choose which trilateral word or scripture you will use.

Let's suppose you are choosing the path of meditation to transcend this spirit of fear. One such *trilateral scripture* that fits with the spiritual consciousness of *anxiety or fear* might be, **"Fear not/ for I Am/ with you" {Isaiah 41:10}.**

Phase 3b: If planning to practice Mindfulness only.

If you are going to simply engage in the practice of Mindfulness surrounding the presence of anxiety, then you would use this scripture as a center of focus- surrounding awareness of this feeling. Focusing on the words of this scripture *(Isaiah 41:10)* and repeating the words of this scripture in its *trilateral cadence* will slowly help to dissipate the feelings of *fear and anxiety*. (Try it now- say the scripture 3 times slowly in the suggested trilateral cadence- "Fear not/ for I Am/ with you.")

Phase 3c: If planning to proceed with the formal practice of Meditation.

If, however, your plan is to proceed with the formal practice of Meditation, then this scripture will only be the first step in the process.

The purpose of this trilateral scripture can be utilized as your anchoring scripture, or mantra, for acknowledging your presence of being in a lower realm of spiritual consciousness.

Your desire, during the meditation process, however, will be to move out of Lower Spiritual Consciousness (LSC) to Higher Spiritual Consciousness (HSC).

The Mindfulness and Meditation Practice- Overview of The Seven Realms

The Formal Mindfulness and Meditation Practice	Identify- Choose-Activate- Transition and Transcend	Examples
Anchoring	Find Your Inner Vibration	The Hum/ Humming
Opening Mantra	Finding Your Focus	The Amen
Centering	Connecting to Spirit	The Breath
STEP 1	Identify Your Present Spiritual Realm	Lower Spiritual Consciousness Realms (LSC)
Phase 1	Identify Your Present TFEs	Fear/ Anxiety
Phase 2	Identify The Realm of Your Present TFE	The 5th Spiritual Realm
Phase 3	Choose the Practice of Mindfulness or Meditation	Choose Meditation
- Phase 3a	Choose a trilateral word or scripture	Isaiah 41:10
- Phase 3b	If Mindfulness only- focus on chosen trilateral word or scripture	'Fear not…"
- Phase 3c	If Meditation- enter the formal Meditation practice	'Fear not for I am with you'
STEP 2	Transcend to The 4th Realm (MSC)	Middle Spiritual Consciousness Realm (MSC)
Phase 1	Transition Your Focus from LSC to MSC	Become aware of the Fear/ Anxiety
Phase 2	Activate Your Spiritual Energy	Redirect your Spiritual Energy towards HSC
Phase 3	Decide on the trilateral scripture for MSC	Romans 12:2-'And do not be conformed…'
STEP 3	Transition to The Realms of HSC	Higher Spiritual Consciousness Realms (HSC)
Phase 1	Direct Your Spiritual Energy to HSC	Direct Your Spiritual Energy to Transcend to HSC
Phase 2	Choose which Realm of HSC you wish to attain	The 1st Realm- The Realm of The Trinity
Phase 3	Choose Your Trilateral Word or Scripture	Psalm 46:10- 'Be still and know that I Am God'

The Mindfulness and Meditation Practice- Overview of The Seven Realms

An Overview of How to Use 'The7Realms' Mindfulness and Meditation Practice- STEP 2:

STEP 2: Transition/Transcend to The Realm of Middle Spiritual Consciousness (MSC)- **The 4th Realm of Spiritual Consciousness- The Realm of Mind, Body, and Soul**

Phase 1: Transcend to from Lower Spiritual Consciousness to Middle Spiritual Consciousness

To accomplish this, you must redirect your spiritual focus away from the thoughts of fear and anxiety to transcend to the realm of Middle Spiritual Consciousness.

In the meditation process of 'The7Realms', you will often use MSC as your transition zone from Lower Spiritual Consciousness (LSC) to Higher Spiritual Consciousness (HSC).

Phase 2: Activate your Spiritual Energy- The Energy of Mind, Body, and Soul

You can activate your conscious Spiritual Energy to shift from this lower consciousness realm to the middle consciousness realm- The 4th Realm- The Realm of Mind, Body, and Soul - using the meditation techniques taught in 'The7Realms'.

Phase 3: Decide on a scripture for the Middle Consciousness Realm

For now, simply decide on the next trilateral scripture- one associated with the middle consciousness realm.

One of my favorite trilateral scriptures for moving through The 4th Realm, or The Realm of Middle Spiritual Consciousness (MSC), is **Romans 12:2- *"And do not be conformed to this world/ but be transformed/ by the renewing of your mind..."***. This anchoring scriptural mantra allows me to initiate a realm of awakening consciousness.

This realm of awakening consciousness allows the transitioning of my thought process to prepare for a move to higher consciousness. This is the definition of middle consciousness. This transition is a key element in the process of Biblical Meditation in 'The7Realms'.

The Mindfulness and Meditation Practice- Overview of The Seven Realms

The Formal Mindfulness and Meditation Practice	Identify- Choose-Activate- Transition and Transcend	Examples
Anchoring	Find Your Inner Vibration	The Hum/ Humming
Opening Mantra	Finding Your Focus	The Amen
Centering	Connecting to Spirit	The Breath
STEP 1	Identify Your Present Spiritual Realm	Lower Spiritual Consciousness Realms (LSC)
Phase 1	Identify Your Present TFEs	Fear/ Anxiety
Phase 2	Identify The Realm of Your Present TFE	The 5th Spiritual Realm
Phase 3	Choose the Practice of Mindfulness or Meditation	Choose Meditation
- Phase 3a	Choose a trilateral word or scripture	Isaiah 41:10
- Phase 3b	If Mindfulness only- focus on chosen trilateral word or scripture	'Fear not…"
- Phase 3c	If Meditation- enter the formal Meditation practice	'Fear not for I am with you'
STEP 2	Transcend to The 4th Realm (MSC)	Middle Spiritual Consciousness Realm (MSC)
Phase 1	Transition Your Focus from LSC to MSC	Become aware of the Fear/ Anxiety
Phase 2	Activate Your Spiritual Energy	Redirect your Spiritual Energy towards HSC
Phase 3	Decide on the trilateral scripture for MSC	Romans 12:2-'And do not be conformed…'
STEP 3	Transition to The Realms of HSC	Higher Spiritual Consciousness Realms (HSC)
Phase 1	Direct Your Spiritual Energy to HSC	Direct Your Spiritual Energy to Transcend to HSC
Phase 2	Choose which Realm of HSC you wish to attain	The 1st Realm- The Realm of The Trinity
Phase 3	Choose Your Trilateral Word or Scripture	Psalm 46:10- 'Be still and know that I Am God'

The Mindfulness and Meditation Practice- Overview of The Seven Realms

An Overview of How to Use 'The7Realms' Mindfulness and Meditation Practice- STEP 3:

STEP 3: Final Step: Time to Transition to The Realms of Higher Spiritual Consciousness

Phase 1: Direct Your Spiritual Energy to Transcend to Higher Spiritual Consciousness:

From middle consciousness I have **3 options (or realms)** to choose from to transition to higher spiritual consciousness:

1. I could choose to go to the next realm, The 3rd Realm- The Realm of Manifestation- Ask, Seek, and Knock.
2. Or I could choose The 2nd Realm- The Realm of The Fruit of The Spirit- Love, Peace, and Joy.
3. Or I could even transcend immediately to the highest realm, The 1st Realm- The Realm of The Trinity- God the Father, God the Son, and God the Holy Spirit.

Phase 2: Choosing the Realm- (Example- Choosing The Highest Realm)

Let's assume I choose to go immediately to the highest realm- **The 1st Realm of Spiritual Consciousness- The Realm of The Trinity- God the Father, God the Son, and God the Holy Spirit.** The Realm of The Trinity is the highest of the seven realms and represents the state of God consciousness. Reaching this realm is a prerequisite to attain oneness with The I AM and experience the fullness of God in us.

Phase 3: Choose Your Trilateral Word or Scripture.

Once you choose your realm, now you must choose a scripture that corresponds to that realm. If I choose the highest realm, I might choose the simple trilateral scripture which I believe is one of the most powerful scriptures in all the Bible. ***"Be still/ and know/ that I Am God." {Psalm 46:10}.*** This scripture contains the spiritual energy and power you would need to transition to the highest level of spiritual consciousness- God-consciousness.

The Mindfulness and Meditation Practice- Overview of The Seven Realms

The Formal Mindfulness and Meditation Practice	Identify- Choose-Activate-Transition and Transcend	Examples
Anchoring	Find Your Inner Vibration	The Hum/ Humming
Opening Mantra	Finding Your Focus	The Amen
Centering	Connecting to Spirit	The Breath
STEP 1	Identify Your Present Spiritual Realm	Lower Spiritual Consciousness Realms (LSC)
Phase 1	Identify Your Present TFEs	Fear/ Anxiety
Phase 2	Identify The Realm of Your Present TFE	The 5th Spiritual Realm
Phase 3	Choose the Practice of Mindfulness or Meditation	Choose Meditation
- Phase 3a	Choose a trilateral word or scripture	Isaiah 41:10
- Phase 3b	If Mindfulness only- focus on chosen trilateral word or scripture	'Fear not…"
- Phase 3c	If Meditation- enter the formal Meditation practice	'Fear not for I am with you'
STEP 2	Transcend to The 4th Realm (MSC)	Middle Spiritual Consciousness Realm (MSC)
Phase 1	Transition Your Focus from LSC to MSC	Become aware of the Fear/ Anxiety
Phase 2	Activate Your Spiritual Energy	Redirect your Spiritual Energy towards HSC
Phase 3	Decide on the trilateral scripture for MSC	Romans 12:2-'And do not be conformed…'
STEP 3	Transition to The Realms of HSC	Higher Spiritual Consciousness Realms (HSC)
Phase 1	Direct Your Spiritual Energy to HSC	Direct Your Spiritual Energy to Transcend to HSC
Phase 2	Choose which Realm of HSC you wish to attain	The 1st Realm- The Realm of The Trinity
Phase 3	Choose Your Trilateral Word or Scripture	Psalm 46:10- 'Be still and know that I Am God'

The Mindfulness and Meditation Practice - Overview of The Seven Realms

An Overview of How to Use 'The7Realms' Mindfulness and Meditation Practice- The Closing:

The Closing Meditation

Once I have engaged and embraced the **full enlightenment of this scripture** and its continued meaning in the specific realm of spiritual consciousness, I have completed the journey.

First, I **correctly identify** which Thought, Feeling, and/or Emotion (TFE) I presently exist within. In this case – Anxiety/ Fear **(STEP 1)**. Anxiety exists in **Lower Spiritual Consciousness-LSC**.

Once I identify my correct realm of present existence (by my TFE- anxiety), I can initiate the **transformation of thought** through my mind **(Middle Spiritual Consciousness- MSC)** to **a state of conscious awareness (STEP 2)**.

Lastly, in the practice of meditation in 'The7Realms', I will **direct the focus of my Spiritual Energy** onto the **Realm of Higher Spiritual Consciousness- HSC (STEP 3)**, using the chosen trilateral scripture for higher consciousness *'Be still and know that I Am God'*- God consciousness.

Since, the realms of spiritual consciousness are based on the practice that when we purposefully direct our spiritual energy, in the form of **attention (focused prayer)** and **intention (scriptural meditation),** we can **ascend to higher consciousness**.

By doing so we achieve the transcendental reality of our spiritual being-ness (spiritual consciousness), and **we conspire with God to bring our true Self closer to the I AM.**

12.4- Examples of Anchoring Prayer(s)- Let's Begin...

Examples of Anchoring Prayer(s):

The <u>first choice</u> for an Anchoring Prayer in 'The7Realms'

The Lord's Prayer. Matthew 6:9-13

⁹ In this manner, therefore, pray:
Our Father in heaven,
Hallowed be Your name.

¹⁰ Your kingdom come.

Your will be done.

On earth as it is in heaven.

¹¹ Give us this day our daily bread.

¹² And forgive us our debts,
As we forgive our debtors.

¹³ And do not lead us into temptation,

But deliver us from the evil one.

[a]For Yours is the kingdom and the power and the glory forever. Amen.

Examples of Anchoring Prayer(s):

The <u>second choice</u> for an Anchoring Prayer in "The7Realms'

The Lord the Shepherd of His People- A Psalm of David. Psalm 23: 1-6

23 The Lord *is* my shepherd; I shall not [a]want.

² He makes me to lie down in [b]green pastures;
He leads me beside the [c]still waters.

³ He restores my soul;

He leads me in the paths of righteousness for His name's sake.

⁴ Yea, though I walk through the valley of the shadow of death,
I will fear no evil;

For You *are* with me; Your rod and Your staff, they comfort me.

⁵ You prepare a table before me in the presence of my enemies;
You anoint my head with oil; My cup runs over.

⁶ Surely goodness and mercy shall follow me all the days of my life;
And I will [d]dwell in the house of the Lord
[e]Forever.

12.5- The Comprehensive Practice of 'The7Realms'-STEP 1- Identify the Realm of Spiritual Consciousness You Exist in Now and Start the Meditation Process Here

The Comprehensive Practice of 'The7Realms'

Begin STEP 1

The Hum- Finding Your Inner Vibration

"Humm…"

"Humm…"

"Humm…"

The Amen- Opening Biblical Meditation Mantra

"Amen…."

"Amen…."

"Amen…."

The Breath- Opening Deep Breathing for Biblical Meditation

Deep breath in… hold for 3 seconds.

Exhale out…" The Breath of God".

Deep breath in… hold for 3 seconds.

Exhale out…" The Breath of Spirit"

Deep breath in… hold for 3 seconds.

Exhale out…" The Breath of Life"

The Comprehensive Practice of 'The7Realms'

Phase 1 -Establish where you are in a Lower Consciousness state- your subconscious, or even unconscious, spiritual state:

- is it Condemnation, Fear or Worry?

- is it Hatred, Anger or Doubt?

- is it internal, External or Mental/Psychological Disease?

Phase 2- Choose a 'trilateral' meditation scripture that speaks to your level of subconscious spiritual unwellness:

(for instance)

If your subconscious spiritual wellness state is 'Fear', you could choose- *Isaiah 41:10 NKJV.*

"Fear not for I AM with you."

Phase 3- This 'trilateral' scripture is to be prayed out loud three times in three different formats:

The first format is the normal cadence of scripture.

"Fear not for I AM with you."

"Fear not for I AM with you."

"Fear not for I AM with you."

The second format is the 'trilateral' cadence of scripture.

"Fear not/ for I AM/ with you."

"Fear not/ for I AM/ with you."

"Fear not/ for I AM/ with you."

The Comprehensive Practice of 'The7Realms'

The third format is the personalized 'trilateral' cadence of scripture.

"Fear not {Ryan}/ for I AM/ with you."

"Fear not {Ryan}/ for I AM/ with you."

"Fear not {Ryan}/ for I AM/ with you."

The Closing Biblical Meditation Mantra

Amen… "Lord, I believe." *Mark 9:24* NKJV

Amen… "Lord, help my unbelief." *Mark 9:24* NKJV

Amen… "But speak the Word only and thy servant shall be healed." *Matt 8:8* KJV

The Mindfulness and Meditation Practice- Overview of The Seven Realms

The Formal Mindfulness and Meditation Practice	Identify- Choose-Activate-Transition and Transcend	Examples
Anchoring	Find Your Inner Vibration	The Hum/ Humming
Opening Mantra	Finding Your Focus	The Amen
Centering	Connecting to Spirit	The Breath
STEP 1	Identify Your Present Spiritual Realm	Lower Spiritual Consciousness Realms (LSC)
Phase 1	Identify Your Present TFEs	Fear/ Anxiety
Phase 2	Identify The Realm of Your Present TFE	The 5th Spiritual Realm
Phase 3	Choose the Practice of Mindfulness or Meditation	Choose Meditation
- Phase 3a	Choose a trilateral word or scripture	Isaiah 41:10
- Phase 3b	If Mindfulness only- focus on chosen trilateral word or scripture	'Fear not…"
- Phase 3c	If Meditation- enter the formal Meditation practice	'Fear not for I am with you'
STEP 2	Transcend to The 4th Realm (MSC)	Middle Spiritual Consciousness Realm (MSC)
Phase 1	Transition Your Focus from LSC to MSC	Become aware of the Fear/ Anxiety
Phase 2	Activate Your Spiritual Energy	Redirect your Spiritual Energy towards HSC
Phase 3	Decide on the trilateral scripture for MSC	Romans 12:2-'And do not be conformed…'
STEP 3	Transition to The Realms of HSC	Higher Spiritual Consciousness Realms (HSC)
Phase 1	Direct Your Spiritual Energy to HSC	Direct Your Spiritual Energy to Transcend to HSC
Phase 2	Choose which Realm of HSC you wish to attain	The 1st Realm- The Realm of The Trinity
Phase 3	Choose Your Trilateral Word or Scripture	Psalm 46:10- 'Be still and know that I Am God'

12.6- The Comprehensive Practice of 'The7Realms'-STEP 2 - Transition to The Realm of Middle Consciousness- Becoming Conscious

The Comprehensive Practice of 'The7Realms'

Begin STEP 2

The Hum- Finding Your Inner Vibration

"Humm…"

"Humm…"

"Humm…"

The Amen- Opening Biblical Meditation Mantra

"Amen…."

"Amen…."

"Amen…."

The Breath- Opening Deep Breathing for Biblical Meditation

Deep breath in… hold for 3 seconds.

Exhale out…" The Breath of God".

Deep breath in… hold for 3 seconds.

Exhale out…" The Breath of Spirit"

Deep breath in… hold for 3 seconds.

Exhale out…" The Breath of Life"

The Comprehensive Practice of 'The7Realms'

Phase 1- moves you to into the Middle Consciousness Realm- The 4th Realm:

- The Realm of Mind, Body, and Soul

This is the transitional realm that allows you to begin your transcendental rise to Higher Consciousness:

So, in this Phase your focus is always from Mind, Body, and Soul.

Phase 2- Choose a 'trilateral' meditation scripture that helps to move you to a state of Middle Consciousness. (for instance)

For Middle Consciousness you could choose- **Romans 12:2** NKJV.

"And do not be conformed to this world, but be transformed by the renewing of your mind, that you may prove what is that good and acceptable and perfect will of God."

Phase 3- This 'trilateral' scripture is to be prayed out loud three times in three different formats:

The first format is the normal cadence of scripture.

"And do not be conformed to this world, but be transformed by the renewing of your mind, that you may prove what is that good and acceptable and perfect will of God."

"And do not be conformed to this world, but be transformed by the renewing of your mind, that you may prove what is that good and acceptable and perfect will of God."

"And do not be conformed to this world, but be transformed by the renewing of your mind, that you may prove what is that good and acceptable and perfect will of God."

The Comprehensive Practice of 'The7Realms'

The second format is the 'trilateral' cadence of scripture.

"And do not be conformed to this world/ but be transformed by the renewing of your mind/ that you may prove what is that good and acceptable and perfect will of God."

"And do not be conformed to this world/ but be transformed by the renewing of your mind/ that you may prove what is that good and acceptable and perfect will of God."

"And do not be conformed to this world/ but be transformed by the renewing of your mind/ that you may prove what is that good and acceptable and perfect will of God."

The third format is the personalized 'trilateral' cadence of scripture.

"And do not be conformed to this world {Ryan} / but be transformed by the renewing of your mind/ that you may prove what is that good and acceptable and perfect will of God."

"And do not be conformed to this world {Ryan} / but be transformed by the renewing of your mind/ that you may prove what is that good and acceptable and perfect will of God."

"And do not be conformed to this world {Ryan}/ but be transformed by the renewing of your mind/ that you may prove what is that good and acceptable and perfect will of God."

The Closing Biblical Meditation Mantra

Amen… "Lord, I believe." *Mark 9:24* NKJV

Amen… "Lord, help my unbelief." *Mark 9:24* NKJV

Amen… "But speak the Word only and thy servant shall be healed." *Matt 8:8* KJV

The Mindfulness and Meditation Practice- Overview of The Seven Realms

The Formal Mindfulness and Meditation Practice	Identify- Choose-Activate- Transition and Transcend	Examples
Anchoring	Find Your Inner Vibration	The Hum/ Humming
Opening Mantra	Finding Your Focus	The Amen
Centering	Connecting to Spirit	The Breath
STEP 1	Identify Your Present Spiritual Realm	Lower Spiritual Consciousness Realms (LSC)
Phase 1	Identify Your Present TFEs	Fear/ Anxiety
Phase 2	Identify The Realm of Your Present TFE	The 5th Spiritual Realm
Phase 3	Choose the Practice of Mindfulness or Meditation	Choose Meditation
- Phase 3a	Choose a trilateral word or scripture	Isaiah 41:10
- Phase 3b	If Mindfulness only- focus on chosen trilateral word or scripture	'Fear not..."
- Phase 3c	If Meditation- enter the formal Meditation practice	'Fear not for I am with you'
STEP 2	Transcend to The 4th Realm (MSC)	Middle Spiritual Consciousness Realm (MSC)
Phase 1	Transition Your Focus from LSC to MSC	Become aware of the Fear/ Anxiety
Phase 2	Activate Your Spiritual Energy	Redirect your Spiritual Energy towards HSC
Phase 3	Decide on the trilateral scripture for MSC	Romans 12:2-'And do not be conformed...'
STEP 3	Transition to The Realms of HSC	Higher Spiritual Consciousness Realms (HSC)
Phase 1	Direct Your Spiritual Energy to HSC	Direct Your Spiritual Energy to Transcend to HSC
Phase 2	Choose which Realm of HSC you wish to attain	The 1st Realm- The Realm of The Trinity
Phase 3	Choose Your Trilateral Word or Scripture	Psalm 46:10- 'Be still and know that I Am God'

12.7- The Comprehensive Practice of 'The7Realms'-STEP 3- Final Step: Transcend- Choose Which Realm of Higher Consciousness You Wish to Attain and Transcend to this Realm

The Comprehensive Practice of 'The7Realms'

Begin STEP 3

The Hum- Finding Your Inner Vibration

"Humm…"

"Humm…"

"Humm…"

The Amen- Opening Biblical Meditation Mantra

"Amen…."

"Amen…."

"Amen…."

The Breath- Deep Breathing for Biblical Meditation

Deep breath in… hold for 3 seconds.

Exhale out…" The Breath of God".

Deep breath in… hold for 3 seconds.

Exhale out…" The Breath of Spirit"

Deep breath in… hold for 3 seconds.

Exhale out…" The Breath of Life"

The Comprehensive Practice of 'The7Realms'

Begin STEP 3

Phase 1- Establish where you want to transcend to for your targeted Higher Consciousness state:

- is it The Realm of The Trinity- God the Father, God the Son and God the Holy Spirit?

- is it The Realm of The Fruit of The Spirit- Love, Peace, and Joy?

- is it The Realm of Manifestation- Ask, Seek and Knock?

Phase 2- Choose a 'trilateral' meditation scripture that speaks to the level of Higher Consciousness you wish to achieve:

(for instance)

If your Higher Consciousness goal/target is for the highest state of Spiritual Wellness- The Trinity- you might choose the following scripture from *Psalm 46:10* NKJV:

"Be still and know that I AM God;"

Phase 3- This 'trilateral' scripture is to be prayed out loud three times in three different formats:

The first format is the normal cadence of scripture.

"Be still and know that I AM God;"

"Be still and know that I AM God;"

"Be still and know that I AM God;"

The Comprehensive Practice of 'The7Realms'

<u>The second format is the 'trilateral' cadence of scripture.</u>

"Be still/ and know that/ I AM God;"

"Be still/ and know that/ I AM God;"

"Be still/ and know that/ I AM God;"

<u>The third format is the personalized 'trilateral' I cadence of scripture.</u>

"Be still {Ryan}/ and know that/ I AM God;"

"Be still {Ryan}/ and know that/ I AM God;"

"Be still {Ryan}/ and know that/ I AM God;"

The Closing Biblical Meditation Mantra

Amen… "Lord, I believe." **Mark 9:24** NKJV

Amen… "Lord, help my unbelief." **Mark 9:24** NKJV

Amen… "But speak the Word only and thy servant shall be healed." **Matt 8:8** KJV

The Mindfulness and Meditation Practice - Overview of The Seven Realms

The Formal Mindfulness and Meditation Practice	Identify- Choose-Activate-Transition and Transcend	Examples
Anchoring	Find Your Inner Vibration	The Hum/ Humming
Opening Mantra	Finding Your Focus	The Amen
Centering	Connecting to Spirit	The Breath
STEP 1	Identify Your Present Spiritual Realm	Lower Spiritual Consciousness Realms (LSC)
Phase 1	Identify Your Present TFEs	Fear/ Anxiety
Phase 2	Identify The Realm of Your Present TFE	The 5th Spiritual Realm
Phase 3	Choose the Practice of Mindfulness or Meditation	Choose Meditation
- Phase 3a	Choose a trilateral word or scripture	Isaiah 41:10
- Phase 3b	If Mindfulness only- focus on chosen trilateral word or scripture	'Fear not...'
- Phase 3c	If Meditation- enter the formal Meditation practice	'Fear not for I am with you'
STEP 2	Transcend to The 4th Realm (MSC)	Middle Spiritual Consciousness Realm (MSC)
Phase 1	Transition Your Focus from LSC to MSC	Become aware of the Fear/ Anxiety
Phase 2	Activate Your Spiritual Energy	Redirect your Spiritual Energy towards HSC
Phase 3	Decide on the trilateral scripture for MSC	Romans 12:2-'And do not be conformed...'
STEP 3	Transition to The Realms of HSC	Higher Spiritual Consciousness Realms (HSC)
Phase 1	Direct Your Spiritual Energy to HSC	Direct Your Spiritual Energy to Transcend to HSC
Phase 2	Choose which Realm of HSC you wish to attain	The 1st Realm- The Realm of The Trinity
Phase 3	Choose Your Trilateral Word or Scripture	Psalm 46:10- 'Be still and know that I Am God'

Questions for Week 12/Lesson 12

Week 12: Day 1

Let's review. Name **The Seven Trilateral Realms of Spiritual Consciousness**.

Week 12: Day 2

What are the **3 Levels of Spiritual Consciousness** in'The7Realms'?

Week 12: Day 3

What are is one example of an **Opening Prayer** for 'The7Realms'?

Week 12: Day 4

What is STEP 1 in the formal Mindfulness and Meditation practice of 'The7Realms'? Describe the 3 Phases under STEP 1.

Week 12: Day 5

What is STEP 2 in the formal Mindfulness and Meditation practice of 'The7Realms'? Describe the 3 Phases under STEP 2.

Week 12: Day 6

What is STEP 3 in the formal Mindfulness and Meditation practice of 'The7Realms'? Describe the 3 Phases under STEP 3.

Week 12: Day 7

How would you describe the final goal of the 3 STEP process? What should we identify in the 1st STEP? What is the middle STEP entail? What should we hope to accomplish in the 3rd STEP?

Ryan C. Neal, MD

In Closing: **Uncovering the Patterns of Trilateral Words in The Bible**

In Closing- Uncovering the Patterns of Trilateral Words in The Bible

The Gift of 'The7Realms'

In this transformational workbook, **The Seven Trilateral Realms of Spiritual Consciousness,** I share my remarkable finding of a spiritual pathway leading to higher consciousness through biblical meditation. 'The7Realms' is the unique discovery of a distinctive correlation between spiritual wellness, spiritual consciousness, and the words of the Bible.

I believe that the patterns I observed in 'The7Realms' were presented to me as a divine gift. I believe I was given the task to explain these patterns as a divine purpose for my life. In this workbook, I reveal my vision of how particular words and scriptures of the Bible relate to the tenets of spiritual consciousness.

I have always believed that every word and every scripture in the Bible had a distinctive meaning and unique significance. As I studied some of the most used words of the Bible, I began to believe that they held an even greater importance.

I even imagined, or possibly hoped, that these recurring words and scriptures might hold the secret to achieving higher consciousness, or more specifically, the consciousness of God.

The Study of The Word

As I studied these words more intently, the distinctive patterns became more evident. As the distinctive *trilateral* patterns were exposed, I drew them out on paper as triangles. Physically seeing the patterns as shapes allowed me to better visualize them and separate them into specific planes. I believed these shapes or planes represented realms of spiritual thoughts, or spiritual consciousness.

As I arranged them into different realms of spiritual consciousness, it became even more clear to me that these biblical patterns were indeed outlining a structure for something. I came to believe this structure represented an outline of spiritual consciousness.

In Closing- Uncovering the Patterns of Trilateral Words in The Bible

And so, I wondered if these newly uncovered patterns, in this newly discovered outline, might somehow expose a pathway to higher consciousness.

If so, I hypothesized that the best way to access this pathway would be through prayer and meditation. Specifically, prayer and meditation centered around these distinct trilateral words in these distinct trilateral patterns.

The Trilateral Words and Scriptures

I would therefore spend the next three decades of my life seeking to discern the hidden connection between these trilateral words and scriptures of the Bible and the potential of these words to achieve higher consciousness.

I researched countless perspectives regarding the definitions, the interpretations, and the meaning behind the recurring trilateral words I found in the Bible. I researched numerous trilateral words such as *love, peace,* and *joy; mercy, grace,* and *hope;* and *ask, seek,* and *knock*. I studied countless precepts such as *"love thy neighbor"*, *"meditate on The Word"*, *"be not afraid"*, and *"do not worry"*.

I read theological and philosophical interpretations regarding scriptural references to *God, Jesus Christ,* and *The Holy Spirit; prayer, supplication,* and *meditation;* as well as the opposing references of *fear, worry,* and *doubt: condemnation, hatred,* and *sin;* and *sickness, disease,* and even *death.*

My evolving awareness of this apparent, if not purposeful use of certain recurring words and scriptural themes mixed with my gift for pattern recognition, steered me towards my pursuit of a more careful examination of these words.

I contemplated various biblical teachings and listened to reputable pastors, priests, and other biblical scholars illuminate different verses, passages, and scriptures, always looking for a pattern, a theme or even a system or formula to better establish the potential mysteries hidden in these recurring words. I noticed that many of the most memorable and well-quoted scriptures had a 3-part, or trilateral, cadence.

In Closing- Uncovering the Patterns of Trilateral Words in The Bible

The Spiritual Significance of the Number 3

My keen awareness of the biblical and spiritual significance of the number 3 once again came to light in these trilateral scriptures representing- holiness, wholeness, and perfection.

I gradually uncovered more and more trilateral words as I explored the Bible. These and other frequently appearing words seemed to occur together in the different gospels throughout the Bible.

Scriptures such as: *In the beginning there was the Word, and the Word was with God, and the Word was God. (John 1:1); Ask and it shall be given, seek and ye shall find, knock and the door will be opened. (Matt 7:7-8);* and *Be still and know that I am God. (Psalm 46:10)*, began to illuminate the truth of this trilateral concept and drove me to delve even further.

A Newfound Path to Spiritual Consciousness

Thus, through this perception of trilateral pattern recognition, these words and scriptures began to take on a new meaning and synergy. These recurring words, placed in a certain order and structural organization, unveiled a surprising new energy and power concealed in the words of the Bible.

The simple precepts outlined in this work reveals a newly discovered, multi-dimensional, ordering system of 84 *trilateral* words and scriptures from the Bible, hidden in specific patterns. These patterns reveal the seven realms of spiritual consciousness.

This noteworthy revelation uncovers a distinctive spiritual path, outlined in 'The7Realms', and invites you to travel along this new path to higher spiritual consciousness *(Christian Mindfulness)*, by way of focused prayer on the specifically outlined trilateral words and scriptures of the Bible (*Biblical Meditation*).

In Closing- Uncovering the Patterns of Trilateral Words in The Bible

I called this new discovery **The Seven Trilateral Realms of Spiritual Consciousness.** And so 'The7Realms' was born. I hope you enjoyed this workbook and the lessons enclosed. Please look forward to the upcoming book by the same title. Peace and love.
-RC Neal

"The one thing I want from God, the thing I seek most of all, is the privilege of **meditating in his Temple, living in his presence every day of my life***, delighting in his incomparable perfections and glory." {Psalm 27:4-- The Living Bible}*

Made in United States
Troutdale, OR
12/31/2024